Us
and
Them

A MEMOIR
OF TRIBES
AND TRIBULATIONS

SID TAFLER

NETBC
PUBLISHING

VICTORIA, CANADA

Net B.C. Publishing Ltd.
www.netbc.com

Library and Archives Canada Cataloguing in Publication Data

Tafler, Sid 1947–
    Us and them : a memoir of tribes and tribulations / Sid Tafler.

ISBN 0–9781017–0–7

    1. Tafler, Sid, 1947–. 2. Tafler family. 3. Canada—History.
4. Canada—Genealogy. I. Title.

FC27.T34 2006   920.71'0971   C2006-902762-5

Design: Arifin Graham, Alaris Design
Front cover photo: Abe Tafler
Back cover photo and photo page 28: Tony Bounsall
Front cover hand-colouring and photo page 207: Brett Lowther

Printed and bound in Canada by Hignell Book Printing
Printed on 100 per cent recycled, chlorine-free paper

to Jennifer

and

to Sarah

CONTENTS

ACKNOWLEDGEMENTS

I offer gratitude to those who reviewed this work
and provided helpful comments and suggestions: Harry
Brechner, Ross Crockford, Danda Humphreys, Kevin
Gillese, Dan Nevin, Ken Roueche, Andrew Struthers,
Gitta Tafler, Marvin Tafler, Penny Tennenhouse and
Star Weiss. I received invaluable advice and assistance
from Carolyn Bateman, a patient and insightful editor,
and for this I offer deep gratitude as well. Bill Johnstone
edited a later draft with great skill and diligence and
helped guide me into home port, for which I am grateful.
I would like to thank Charles Tidler for inspiration
and encouragement. Jennifer Tafler and Sarah Tafler
have given me the greatest gifts, love and support beyond
measure. Special thanks as well to my teachers at all levels
of learning. I have been fortunate to have had many
who offered great wisdom, some of which I absorbed
and remembered. Among the most important were
Louis and Manya Shetzer, who taught me life lessons
at their kitchen table.

PART ONE
CHILD

I

SARAH

The young, dark-haired woman is wrapped in white sheets, sweating and gasping. The deep pain wells up in her abdomen and spreads downward over ten, twenty seconds, then subsides. Above her shines a bright metallic light, trained at her body, its reflective glare washing over her eyes. She drifts in and out of consciousness, aware of the passage of time but losing track of the hours.

Around her are blank walls, masked faces and white uniforms that appear and disappear. On the far wall, a clock, black hands and numbers on a white face. Sometimes she sees the hands in a blur, other times she makes sense of them—eight-fifteen, nine-twenty, ten. Is it day or night? Has she been here six hours or twelve? There are injections—the quick swab, the alcohol fume, the pointy jab in her forearm. She loses consciousness, gains it again, swirls in and out as the swells of pain deepen and become more frequent. She moans and thrusts.

Images flash before her eyes: her mother, soft black hair, crinkly smiling eyes, speaking her name to comfort her, "Sarah, Sarah." Then her husband, in grey winter coat and fedora, tall and handsome like Errol Flynn, a flash of black moustache moving with his lips. But she can't hear what he's saying. He bends to kiss her brow, then fades.

The pain is deeper now, unbearable. She cries out. Someone holds her hand, then wipes her brow. Another injection. She drifts in and out. Then suddenly a moment of clarity, a liquid rush through her body, a final thrust, a feeling of deep release. The fierce edge of pain subsides. Her eyes fix on the clock, one hand pointing straight up, the other to the floor: twelve-thirty.

One of the faces is now unmasked, a white cap, green eyes, the mouth smiling, the expression distant, professional. "Congratulations, Mrs. Tafler, you have a little baby boy." She collapses in relief and tears and happiness. She breathes deeply and her eyes close.

In a few moments her mind begins to swirl again. She opens her eyes and moves her tongue inside her mouth, a metallic taste. Oh no, the pain is returning, gathering deep inside, now suddenly as intense as before. It's happening again—the walls, the light, the thrashing and thrusting, drifting between dreaming and waking like a tired swimmer bobbing at the waterline.

Some time later—she can't tell if it's minutes or hours—she has another moment of clarity, then the liquid rush, the thrust, the release, the pain slipping away like a blanket falling from her body. She opens her eyes and her gaze is pulled to the clock. The black pointed hands tell the story as before: twelve-thirty. Then the same nurse appears in white, the same clear green eyes, the same slightly forced smile. Sarah knows the words are coming, but before she can speak, the nurse tells her again: "Congratulations, Mrs. Tafler, you have a little baby boy." This time there is less relief, but there are still tears and happiness mixed with the puzzling recognition of a moment of transformation lived a second time.

A few minutes later, the tall man with the moustache and fedora rushes in, on his lunch break from the office. He had to fight his way through a wild winter storm blowing on the city streets to get to the hospital. "Where's my son?" he asks his exhausted wife. Your son, she thinks. After what I've been through.

I may have been three or four when my mother first told me the story of my birth. The last of three children, I was a curly-haired boy who loved nothing more than his sweet, comforting mother. She and I formed a bond that may have been particular to mother and youngest child, her "baby" as she persisted in calling me into my adult years. We shared a connection that stood secretly but steadfastly against the rest of the world, even the rest of the family. And this story of my birth, this long and painful struggle to bring my life into the world, apparently experienced in a dream-state before it happened, strengthened the bond between us like mortar between bricks.

She suffered and endured and sacrificed for me in labour as she would many times again after I was born. But I suffered as well, evicted in great struggle from my warm floating cocoon inside her body. Of course I had no conscious memory of my birth. But my mother gave it consciousness, telling me the story over and over in childhood, adolescence and adulthood. And so I knew I was born in great difficulty, over a long labour that caused my mother great pain, but that she hoped and endured and finally thrust me into this world—not once but twice—and that she loved me all the more for it. I was born once in her mind, perhaps as a release from the intense pain she was suffering, and born again in physical form in identical detail.

And so I formed my first bond with another human being. I soon found that this bond must be used like a shield against harm from other people. Those people were, ambiguously, people we loved, the three other members of our family.

Can we draw meaning from a difficult birth? Perhaps I didn't want to be born but wanted to stay inside my mother. It was a difficult world to come into, joining a competitive, conflicted family as the youngest, the most vulnerable. My mother had to dream my birth and then experience it, while I held on to the warm protected place inside her. I became a clinging child, dependent on her, trying to maintain or recapture the close connection. I knew the fear of being small in a world of big people, the fear of pain, and most of all the fear of being cast out and abandoned.

2

THE CROSS
ON THE MOUNTAIN

The skinny woman wondered why the big woman who lived on the floor above kept climbing the stairs, day and night. This was much more than the usual chores of bringing in groceries and hauling out garbage. The big woman walked the stairs, from the entrance at the bottom to the top floor, several times a day carrying nothing in her arms.

Finally, the skinny woman couldn't resist asking. She opened the door as the big woman approached the landing.

"Walking again, Mrs. Shetzer?"

Mrs. Shetzer looked up and stopped to catch her breath. "Yes."

"Why do you keep walking?"

"It's this child," she said and gestured at her belly.

"You're expecting?"

"Yes. Again."

The skinny woman arched her brows. "You mean you want to lose your baby?"

"Who can afford another baby? I just had one last year. And my husband isn't working." She started walking on the landing past the skinny woman's door.

"Listen. Come back later, I'll make a mixture for you. It's from the old country, my family's recipe. It will start an early labour."

Mrs. Shetzer turned her head back to the woman. "A mixture? What time?"

"Eight o'clock. After dinner."

"Eight o'clock." She continued walking again and the skinny woman closed her door.

My grandmother Manya took the potion that night and several times more in the coming weeks. It was green and bitter but she forced it down. She walked the stairs, up and down until her feet ached. She even climbed the roads and trails leading up Mount Royal. She took hot baths. She went for car rides, telling the driver to go as fast as possible. But despite all her efforts, she did not miscarry; the child stayed in her belly. She gave birth to a small and beautiful baby, her third child, her only girl, in the late summer of 1916. She never thought of recording the date, and throughout my mother's life she was never sure on which day in August she was born.

As she held the squirming baby in her arms, Manya formed an immediate bond of love that wiped away the rejection of the failed miscarriage. This was her daughter, her girl, her only female family member now that she was separated from her mother and sister back in Russia, who she would never see again. This little girl was to become her soulmate, the closest, dearest love of her life. And like my mother, her mother told her the story of her fated birth over and again.

Like me, Sarah was the last child in a family of two boys and a girl. But while my family was middle class and ascending, hers was desperately poor, often stumbling from one crisis to the next. The 1920s were tough times for a poor immigrant family in Montreal, the 1930s even tougher in the years of the Great Depression. My grandfather Louis spoke little English and could find only sporadic work as a presser of men's suits in the clothing factories on The Main, St. Lawrence Boulevard. He'd have a few weeks' work and then show up one day and find he was laid off or replaced. When he finally had a steady job, the entire factory went out on strike in the early days of union organization in the sweatshops of east-end Montreal.

My mother's family lived in a walk-up on St. Dominique Street, a flat with only a small heater in the hallway to withstand the fierce winter storms that blew across the city. In the coldest weather, the windows and even the inside walls of the family home were covered in frost. The flat had no bath. Sarah and her mother would go to the public baths once a week on women's day, her father and two brothers on men's day.

As a little girl, my mother, already instinctively maternal, yearned for a doll. Her family was too poor to afford toys so my grandmother found a stick and wrapped it in rags. This was Sarah's doll and she cradled and fussed over it like any devoted mother would care for her baby.

My grandmother's constant worry was keeping her family fed. In the old country, the people in her village often faced hunger, sometimes starvation. In Canada, in the tough times during the 1920s and '30s, her family survived on the goodwill of the grocer around the corner, who extended credit over weeks and months. He kept a record book of the money Mrs. Shetzer owed, and she repaid him when she could.

Manya shared her worries with her little girl.

"The rent is due. Where will we get the money?"

"Don't worry, Ma, we'll find it."

"How will we find it?"

"We will, we will."

"Oy, my little one, your father is still on strike."

Suddenly Sarah brightened. "Al is going to start selling fruit. He'll make lots of money."

At the age of thirteen, my mother's oldest brother Al began working for a peddler who sold fruit door to door. And my grandmother managed to scrape together the money to pay the landlord.

From an early age, Sarah became Manya's fellow sufferer who would listen to her troubles and secrets. Sarah was someone you could depend on, who would take on hardship and responsibility to relieve the burden on others. It was a role she would assume over and again in life, as wife, mother, sister-in-law, friend.

As a small girl, she was aware of the ethnic separation and rivalry of her neighbourhood flanking the great commercial artery, St. Lawrence Boulevard. There were French, English, Irish, Italians, and at the bottom of the ladder, the most distrusted and disliked, the Jews.

She knew there were streets to avoid, and she knew she was always safer with one of her brothers by her side.

She played on the sidewalk with her friends, skipping rope. She was turning the rope and she didn't see the young boys approach from down the street. In an instant, one of them pushed her to the ground. As she lay there sprawling, a small girl with black braids, he turned and spat, "Out of the way, Jew."

This her mother also told her: the goyim, the gentiles, are out to get us. They killed us in the old country and they'll kill us here if they get the chance. Stay away from them. And stay away from their cross and their church.

When she went to bed at night in her small, cramped bedroom, from her window she could see the towering metal cross perched on Mount Royal, overlooking and claiming the city. To the goyim, the cross was their holiest symbol, the sign of the promise of salvation and redemption at the core of their religion. To the Jews, it meant persecution, suffering, eternal blame and the horrors of forced conversion.

At night, the cross on the mountain was lit up, visible for miles around, carrying a message to my mother: "We are Christian, Catholic. We put our sign at the highest point in the city. It is the symbol of the suffering and death of our Saviour. And of the blame you carry for killing him."

To Sarah that cross represented the oppression and hatred her people had suffered for centuries, from the Romans who burned the Temple in Jerusalem to the boy on the street who pushed her to the ground. At night in her bedroom she looked out at the huge metal cross, casting its powerful spell, and she spit in the air in defiance.

★

By her late teens, Sarah was a slim, black-haired and strikingly beautiful woman. She was hired as a secretary in her first job at Stella Dress, a women's clothing factory.

But the boss soon chose her to model dresses for buyers and photographers because of her natural poise and grace. She looked familiar, like someone you saw in a movie, and in some social circles in Montreal she was mistaken for an actress trying to conceal her identity. Men of wealth and standing competed to court her. But her beauty could not bear description of her facial features. Her own mother, an earthy matriarch, mocked the idea: "Crooked teeth, a long nose, one eye bigger than the other. And they say she's beautiful." But they were right. Beauty is not a nose or an eye, but the sum of the parts, an expression, an attitude, an "it" that Sarah had and coyly flaunted. That silky raven hair combed away from her brow, that smile and those sparkling eyes, they revealed an inner beauty that burst forth like sunlight flashing through a diamond.

On their second encounter, Abe found Sarah at a house party. They had met some weeks before. She was flattered by his attention but avoided giving him her last name or phone number. She was barely eighteen, demure and unsure of the intentions of this brash young man. He was tall, handsome, self-assured, already a businessman and champion athlete at twenty-one. And he was dating her own best friend and known to be a young man on the prowl. He had remembered this lovely young girl he had met before and had tried to contact her through friends. Now he saw her again as he arrived at the party. Sarah stood in a small circle amid clinking glasses, the fog of tobacco smoke, the rising din of chatter among old friends and new acquaintances. Abe made his way toward her across the room with barely a nod to anyone else.

They talked for a few moments and he led her to another room where they sat down. He lifted her hand, intertwined her fingers with his and fixed her with his gaze. "I've been looking for you since we met. And now that I've found you, I'm never going to let you go." He kissed her, pressing his body close, and her heart fluttered like the wings of a trapped bird. Abe kept true to his promise, for sixty-five years.

They shared a love that was deep, devoted and conflicted. She might have known that a man who would lock her delicate fingers with his big hand at their second meeting, who abandoned her best friend to pursue her, was a man of some complication and control. But she ignored any caution and gave herself fully to his great power, his strength, his devotion, his guiding hand. She lived her life a willing prisoner, overcome by emotional attachment so strong it wiped out all doubts and contradictions.

The Depression extended my parents' courtship for five years. Work was hard to come by and just as hard to keep and their marriage plans kept getting delayed. They both still lived in their parents' homes, which was common practice in those times for unmarried adults. She was twenty-three and he was twenty-six and they were anxious to marry and start a family. In the summer of 1939, they set a date in October.

Full of the heady optimism of a young woman planning her new life, Sarah set about the task of finding a home. She scanned the newspaper ads for apartments for rent and called to make appointments to see them. Several times she was told on the phone that a place was available, but when she arrived a few hours later, it was suddenly taken.

One September evening she found the perfect place on a quiet tree-lined street close to the mountain. She called the landlord and the next day she rushed over to see the apartment. As she approached the building, she saw a sign posted near the door:

NO DOGS

NO CATS

NO JEWS

She stopped at the edge of the sidewalk. She stared at the words for a few moments and then turned and walked away.

When she told me this story years later, I asked her how it felt to see that sign. "Like I'd been kicked in the stomach," she said, grimacing as if she'd been kicked again.

Sarah returned to her mother's home, shaken. She had been born and raised in this country, a productive member of society. She had never broken the law, never even had a parking ticket or dropped litter on the street. She was a beautiful young woman about to get married, to endow her future children, her most precious legacy, to this country. And she was being treated like an outcast with an infectious disease.

That evening in her room she wept as she told Abe about the sign on the building.

He reached out and comforted her. "Don't worry. We'll show them. We'll get a story in the papers."

"It's no use. It's not the only place like that."

"We can't let them do this. We have to fight back."

"I don't want to fight. Why are we living here? Why should we bring up our children here?"

Abe didn't answer.

"Can't we go . . . live in Palestine?"

What a thought. This was 1939, the start of the war. In Palestine, small groups of Jewish *chalutzim*, pioneers, were hand-digging sun-baked soil, clearing swamps and rocks, surrounded by hostile Arab *fellahin*, peasants. They were sleeping in shacks, living on bread and beans, building the future state with their sweat and blood. If she didn't want to fight in Canada, she would face a much worse struggle in Palestine. War clouds were gathering across the Mediterranean in Europe. Hitler was threatening the entire continent and North Africa, the Middle East, the Jews especially. In Montreal, they had extended families, connections, opportunities. Palestine? The moon.

But Abe wouldn't let the humiliation rest. He worked up a scheme with his good friend Flin Flanagan, a cheery Irish dentist, to apply to rent apartments where my mother was turned down. Suddenly, when they saw his face and name, the same places were available. Flin collected a list of these buildings and went to a reporter. Abe got his story in the paper, which shamed the landlords who practised discrimination. He and Sarah rented an apartment on the same tree-lined street as the building with the sign banning pets and Jews. They had a happy time there, a newlywed couple alone together and deeply in love. And eventually, the sign came down.

★

As a little boy in a conflicted world of big people, I stuck to my mother like a fawn to a doe. We spent days alone

together when my father was at work, my older sister
and brother at school. Knowing I was the last, she wanted
me to be her little child for as long as possible. In our
mid-1950s kitchen under fluorescent light, she carefully
rolled out the dough for poppy-seed cookies and spread
it on the Arborite table. I helped her form the cookies
into small shapes by twisting the mouth of a glass against
the thin dough. She created wavy, rectangular shapes with
a rolling cookie cutter. The dog stood under the table,
waiting for a scrap to fall from heaven. I got a spot of
flour on my face and my mother knelt to wipe it away.

She was the keeper of family history, a gifted story-
teller who remembered details and sensations years after
they happened and repeated the same stories time and
again. This day, she recounted the story of my birth. I
listened as she described the clock in the hospital room,
the moment of birth lived and then lived again.

"I wanted to tell the nurse, 'I know what you're going
to say.'"

"Why didn't you, Mummy?"

"I didn't get the chance. She said it just as I was opening my mouth."

"Was it real? Did it really happen?"

"It was like a dream."

Then I looked up and saw the green square clock above
our kitchen sink and thought about the clock on the wall
in the hospital. I knew this woman loved me as much as
any mother did even before I was born, and more so now
that I was her baby. She bent over to slide the cookies
into the oven. She turned and smiled at me. The dog shuffled, nose to the floor. In a few moments, the comforting
smell of baking rose and drifted from the kitchen to spread

through the house. When my brother and sister and father came home, she announced that "we" made cookies. My father smiled, my brother scoffed and we all ate them, even the dog, who got broken and burned ones tossed his way and never complained.

The family was bound by love, but also by a strict hierarchy: my strong-willed father at the top, ruling the household and directing his children with verbal demands or physical force. The children in turn bullied each other, from oldest down to youngest. The last in line, sometimes I picked on the dog.

In our unspoken pact, my mother's role was to protect me, from my father, from my brother and sister, from the greater world beyond which I was only vaguely aware of but knew was a place of fear and danger. Without conscious thought, I felt my mother and I were a unit, a separate inner family that shared a deep attachment and a sense of duty: she gave me love and protection, I gave the sense of being needed by someone small and vulnerable and close to her heart. This was my first notion of us, my mother and I, versus them, the rest of the family. On the cover of this book, the picture tells the story. The young woman in her bathing suit on the beach, smiling at her husband taking the photo. The little boy, his arm around his mother's neck, looking away, wishing the man with the camera hadn't disturbed this moment.

In her five years of courtship with my father, my mother experienced the boisterous camaraderie of his family of six brothers and sisters. Sarah and Abe decided to have a brood of six as well. She had three children in less than five years and was well on her way. The birth order was even the same as my father's family—boy, girl, boy. She was only thirty-one when I was born, but soon after my father became ill with an infected eye and high blood pressure. Six years earlier, Abe's older brother Moe had died of a brain tumour, leaving a wife and newborn daughter. So with my father's health in doubt, Abe and Sarah decided to stop having children, and the dream of a large family faded away. My mother loved babies, little bundles of helplessness she could hold in her arms. Her family became telescoped into half the size she intended, and in a way, her last child became a stand-in for the three she never had.

3

I ALSO REMEMBER

It was a warm spring day on Wiseman Avenue in Outremont, a central Montreal neighbourhood that climbs down the north slope of Mount Royal. The leaves of the tall maples had recently burst from their buds, small and light and fresh green. The sunshine was a welcome gift on the streets of the city recently released from winter's frozen grasp.

On this street two small children played, my sister Gitta, with light brown hair in ringlets, hazel eyes and an earnest expression broken occasionally by laughter, and me, her little brother, a small boy with a tangle of curly dark brown hair. Two years older, perhaps five to my three, she was my guardian and mentor.

We played children's games, exploring, running and jumping over lines in the sidewalk. "Step on a crack, break your mother's back." Horse-drawn carriages delivered milk to our house. The horses relieved themselves on the street and we giggled as we spoke the word "horseshit," our naughty little secret.

Across the street in a large open yard we spotted bright yellow flowers over an expanse of green lawn. This was another part of the world, new unexplored territory. The flowers beckoned and we decided to cross the street. We had never done this before, but Gitta had learned the drill of looking both ways and holding a younger child's hand. She wrapped my small fingers in hers and we stepped out tentatively into the street. There were no cars coming and we rushed across the pavement like scampering lambs. We reached the other side breathless and turned back at a new view of our red brick home framed by mighty maple trunks. There were no houses on this side of the street, just a sweep of lawn surrounding a large domed building. Our excitement grew as we parted a small green hedge and stepped into the yard. We knelt to admire the yellow flowers, little treasures to small children.

"Let's pick some for Mummy," my sister squealed. We began picking, flowers with short stems that barely fit between our thumb and first finger. They formed sticky little bouquets in our hands. Dandelions. Little did we know adults considered them weeds to be destroyed.

We were in reverie in this warm field, comparing our small bouquets, discarding the smallest stems that slipped from our fingers. Then, from across the yard, a large figure dressed in black approached us, a cloak-like garment swirling at either side. In an instant she was upon us. I looked up and saw a prim hooded face behind rimless glasses, a flash of white on her chest. She towered above us like a great black bird inspecting a bug.

"*Va t'en!*" she commanded. Get out! We dropped our flowers and rushed to the sidewalk. My sister held my hand, but as we raced into the street, we forgot to check for cars—luckily there were none. We kept running until we had bounded across the sidewalk and climbed the stairs to the entrance of our house.

The lawn was the backyard of a Roman Catholic church, one of hundreds that dominate villages and neighbourhoods throughout Quebec. The blackbird figure was a nun who lived in the small cloister behind the church. What trouble were these little children causing picking dandelions on the church lawn? It didn't matter. The hedge between the sidewalk and the yard was the border that kept us out of their world. They didn't want us crossing that line and taking anything that belonged to them. Today, weeds on the lawn, tomorrow, maybe the collection box or the cross on top of the church.

My sister and I sat on the front steps of our home. The yard across the street looked far away now, the yellow flowers washed in a sea of green. The black-cloaked woman disappeared inside the low building behind the church. We had been punished for wandering from home, for leaving our side of the street to explore their side. We said nothing, but we knew we wouldn't try that again.

Many years later, I went back to Wiseman Avenue as an adult, a middle-aged man reliving old memories. I knocked on the door of my house and met the woman who lived there and we chatted in French. Her name was Suzanne Lévesque and she worked as a translator. "I used to live here," sounds like a suspicious story coming from a stranger. Then I walked across the street, past the cloister and around to the other side of the church. It looked bigger from here, a grand staircase leading to an elaborate stone entrance. I realized this was the front entrance to the church. I had never seen it before, never managed to walk around to the front of the building when I lived here. And I realized how small my world was when I was a little boy crossing the street to pick flowers on the church lawn.

★

The slogan on Quebec licence plates is *Je me souviens.* I remember. As a motto it pulls at the heart as it invokes the past over the present. Unfinished business. *Je me souviens. Mais de quoi?* Perhaps it's meant to draw Quebecers together in its ambiguity. "I remember my French heritage," or "I remember our defeat, but we will prevail."

I know of no other place in North America so consumed by language and identity. And not just among the French-speaking majority. When I was growing up, there were no "Canadians" in Quebec, meaning people who draw their identity from their country and citizenship. Even though, ironically, French-speakers used the term *Canadiens* to identify and distinguish themselves from everyone else. And there were no Québécois, that term came into vogue later on. There were the French and *les autres*, the others, Them, those who spoke English or other languages. The French, the English, the Greeks, the Italians, were not primarily identified by religion. But we were. Being Jewish is a religion, a culture, an identity. That's a lot of nuance to grasp, but not too much for a child growing up in 1950s Quebec. It was important to know, to identify, to label, to differentiate. You're Us. Or you're not Us. You're Them.

On the streets of lower Outremont, most kids were either French or Jewish, and they were natural enemies.

Levels of mistrust were set in place over generations, re-inforced by anti-Semitic slurs delivered with thunderbolts from the pulpit on Sundays. We were the heirs of genera-tions of persecution, of suspicion between Catholic and Jew, stretching back to obscure villages on the other side of the Atlantic.

One particularly tough kid whose name I forgot would terrorize me whenever he saw me. He was a big, dark-haired boy, often accompanied by other kids who would egg him on or hold him back. I understood only a little French, but it seemed this fearful boy spoke more in gut-tural grunts than words or sentences. He was the classic medieval, wild-eyed terror, the Cossack or Crusader re-born. One day he threatened me on the street, wielding a large piece of broken glass. I ran between two houses, but suddenly my way was blocked by a wire fence and a lilac bush. I turned to face him, fear rippling down my body. He raised the jagged weapon in his hand and growled at me. He stepped closer and closer, slashing at me with the broken glass. I could see my face torn open and started to cry. Then a man appeared in a back win-dow and shouted—"Hey!"—and we ran off in opposite directions.

In later years, I learned about Northern Ireland, one of the most troubled places in the western world, where some Catholics and Protestants hated each other enough to take lives with bombs and bullets. To the outsider, all the Northern Irish looked alike. But they could tell the difference at twenty paces, and that difference was all that mattered. It sounds familiar, I remember thinking. It sounds like Quebec.

In many ways, Quebec was the ultimate place to be

Us, a small Jewish minority living in a nation of French Canadians who struggled to preserve their language and identity in a much bigger entity of Them. Quebec is a history, a psychology, a garrison, a distinctive mentality and culture. French-speaking and Catholic in a vast sea of English-speaking, largely Protestant and British peoples. A place apart, mysterious and unknown to outsiders. A place of passions, piety and sin, hot sultry summers, cold brutal winters. Latin America North.

Inside Quebec lived a French-speaking majority of four million, surrounded by an English-speaking majority in the rest of North America of two hundred million. Further inside Quebec was an English-speaking minority of a million, living mostly in their own regions in and around Montreal. And even deeper within, we were a Jewish minority of a hundred thousand, in our own familiar neighbourhoods—where we were usually the majority. Societies within societies, largely out of touch with each other, like Russian dolls.

In the world I grew up in, you stuck with your own kind, by choice, by necessity or both. We were two generations out of the thousand-year-old ghetto of eastern Europe but still living in the ghetto of the mind. We studied Hebrew and Torah and prayed in *shul* facing Jerusalem, surrounded by French-Canadian Catholics who revered the cross and confessed their sins to the priest. My father even gathered a *minyan*, a quorum of Jews for prayer, on Saturday mornings in the cottage country wilderness in the Laurentian Mountains. We were a strange, exotic people who practised our own secret customs, a tight-knit community so separate some Quebecers thought we had gone extinct in the time of the Bible.

But we fit neatly in the context of mid-century Quebec, in which each ethnic group knew its place and kept watch on the others suspiciously, from a distance.

It was a tribal, bone-deep sense of separation. The French kids spoke a different language, and when they looked at us, we knew the buzz of phrases running together carried the seeds of malice. In my youth, I learned French curses and swear words, but *Juif* on its own invoked more insult than any other word. Forty years later on a visit to Montreal, when I heard small children in the park chattering in French, I felt the familiar spark of hostility flash in my mind.

"Watch out for the Frenchies," my older brother David warned me when I was a small boy.

"Who's the Frenchies?" I asked.

"The bad kids on the street."

My mother overheard us. "Don't say that. They're not Frenchies. They're just children who speak French."

We continued calling them Frenchies, out of earshot of Mom.

I wore a blue and white toque, a woollen cap my mother knitted, just like the French-Canadian kids. I could have passed for one of them—but only to a stranger visiting from somewhere else.

One winter day I was walking home from school, my attention fixed on a big snowball I was forming in my hands. I walked past a barber shop, a newsstand on Van Horne Avenue, cars slopping by, splashing slushy grey snow as they passed. Every few steps, I reached down to a pile of snow and packed another handful onto the ball. By the time I arrived at our street, the snowball was so big I had to cradle it in my arms. This was a prize to show my mother, big enough to be the head of a snowman. Maybe we'd make one when I got home.

Three bigger boys walking on the other side of the street crossed over as soon as they saw me. They approached me with smirks and nudges. *"Hé, toi."* Hey, you. They wanted my snowball. I sheltered it in my arms and tried to get past them. One of them pushed me. *"Donne moi."* Give it to me. He pulled the snowball from my arms. He held it in both hands and his smirk turned to a big smile. Then he shoved it back at me at full speed and it burst in my face. The three of them laughed. *"P'tit Juif."* They walked off chuckling.

I cried, my face cold and red, snow melting down my neck. I was afraid and ashamed. Instead of a snowman's head, I returned home with tears on my cheeks. My mother offered comfort and a glass of hot chocolate. "It's okay, it's just a snowball."

Like the Irish, we could usually smell one another at a distance. But if we couldn't, we would ask. In other parts of the world kids ask each other their names, what games they play, but in Quebec they asked, what's your nationality? Are you English, French, Jewish, Italian or Greek? Tell us so we know how to treat you.

We lived with our own kind, nurtured our identities and kept apart from one another. Each group formed its own unit that separated itself by neighbourhood and class as well as by language and culture.

In my early years I lived in a ring of concentric circles with my family of my father, mother and three children at the centre, surrounded by the greater family of twenty or thirty assorted relatives, a clan connected by heart, mind, telephone line and frequent family visits. The third circle was the greater Jewish community of Montreal, a hundred thousand largely unknown souls whose experience and sentiments we shared. Beyond this were the Jewish people all over the world. And outside these circles were the rest of Montreal, the rest of the country, the rest of the world. The gentiles were strange and foreign, somewhat uncivilized beings thought to vary on a scale between mild hostility and hatred of us Jews.

Because of these strands of connection and the storied legacy of persecution of the Jewish people, our entire lives were immersed in this context. You had to strive to overcome the barriers that stood against you, but nothing you did stood alone as a reflection of your own merits. You were either a credit or honour to your family and the Jewish people—or a failure, a disgrace. The stakes and the bar of achievement were set high. Every Jewish boy should become a great doctor, lawyer or business owner and family man with a loyal wife keeping a good Jewish home. That would reflect well on us and prove our merit to the gentiles, who were thought to be always watching, suspicious of everything we did. We had to try harder, study harder, work harder, keep our noses cleaner than everyone else.

4

ABE'S RING

In the deep, dark night, a roaring explosion that sounds like the earth coming apart blasts through the house, tearing me from sleep. My eyes pop open but there is nothing to see. I clutch my blankets and cry out in fear. Then a sudden flash. A rolling rumble gathers in the distance, moves ominously closer and then explodes around me. This is the very element of terror, a small child alone in the darkness, the world flying apart in deafening blasts.

Then I hear his voice: "It's all right, it's okay." He switches on the bedside lamp and runs his big soft fingers across my brow. My tower of strength and security, my father, is here to rescue me. And now, more than fifty years later, I feel the tears in the corners of my eyes as I remember him.

He is wearing light blue pajamas, sitting on the edge of my bed. I am still weeping, shaking. I can barely talk.

He leans toward me and speaks softly. "It's just a thunderstorm."

I choke out the words, "What's a thunderstorm, Daddy?"

"It's two clouds in the sky, bumping together."

In the distance, two clouds bump together, grumbling at each other.

He raises one great hand above his head. "This is one cloud. It's dark and full of rain. It moves across the sky." He raises his other hand. "And this is the other cloud. It's full of rain and it's moving too."

"Then, suddenly"—he claps his hands together—"the two clouds bump into each other and make a noise called thunder. And the bump lets out all the rain."

The hand-clap breaks the night and pulls me into my father's rational, soothing world of cause and effect. Clouds bumping together, making a sound, nothing to fear. To this day, having heard no better story, I still believe his explanation of thunder. I see his smile in the half-light and lean back on my pillow, wiping my tears. "Go back to sleep now," he whispers. He kisses my brow, switches off the light and leaves the room.

This is the father I would like to remember. Not his tyrannical side, which controlled his family like a drill sergeant and demanded his children reach impossible levels of achievement. But the intensely physical man who loved to work his body, sweat dripping from his brow. A man who saw in his strength the duty to protect the downtrodden, to rescue the helpless.

Who could be more helpless than a weeping child afraid of the thunder? Perhaps a woman rejected by the country of her birth because of a war fought thousands of miles away against the country of her ancestors.

On a bright, hard mid-winter day, the wind whipped down the frozen St. Lawrence River, blowing gusts of swirling loose snow through the streets of Montreal. It was the middle of the war, the early 1940s, five years before my birth. A young woman with straight black hair walked the downtown streets, knocking on office doors, looking for work. She was an accomplished secretary, but no one would give her a job. Every day, doors were closed in her face, or she was told curtly, "We're not hiring now."

The woman had only a cloth coat and street shoes, and she shivered and huddled against the cold, holding her garments close to her body.

She was Japanese-Canadian, one of tens of thousands shunned by their fellow Canadians who feared they would side with their ancestral homeland and form a fifth column in Canada. Many of them were uprooted from their homes on the West Coast and forced to live in camps in the interior of British Columbia. Some made it to cities in Eastern Canada where they struggled to find work.

The woman knocked on the door of my father's business, a small import-export company. He asked her in, her first interview in many days.

Dad, in his crisp navy blue suit and tie, sat behind his desk, fountain pen in hand. The woman, still dressed in her coat and hat, sat opposite him, clutching her purse.

Dad could see she was tense, her hands numb from the raw cold. But he expressed no sympathy and conducted the interview like any other, leaning back in his chair.

"Typing?"

"Sixty words a minute."

"Shorthand?"

"Yes."

"Can you keep books?"

"Yes, sir."

"Do you live in the city?"

"Yes, sir. A rooming house on Dorchester."

"References?"

"Yes, sir." She fumbled in her purse and produced three letters from employers, typed and signed.

Dad examined them. "When can you start?"

"Pardon me?"

"Can you start right away?"

She couldn't believe what she was hearing. "Uh, uh, well, when?"

"How about tomorrow morning, eight thirty?"

"Oh, yes, yes, tomorrow morning, sir."

"My name is Abe." He handed her letters back.

"Ah, yes-sir, Abe-sir, yes."

The woman's name is lost to me, the details of the story come from my mother. She worked for Abe for many years, and if any of his clients objected, he was deaf to it. As someone who faced racism himself, he knew it was his duty to fight it at every turn.

Some years after the war, the woman married and left Abe's employ to start a family. My parents were guests at the wedding. My mother, who remembered the cloth coat, recalled a single detail about the wedding reception: "They served raw fish."

And now I see my father's hands as I look at my own. His fingers were long, strong but delicate, moving softly across the surface of an object he held, like he was trying to see with his touch. His big bald head bent in concentration, his hands feeling, turning, exploring. Those hands that could soothe and comfort or punish, causing pain and fear.

This I remember about my father, over fifty years: he showed no fear, nor doubt, never, not even in the face of death. I was with him on his last day, his body crippled by sickness. He approached the precipice with as much resolve as anything he did in life.

All these years later I wonder how it could be: can a man be fearless and confident about every decision, every circumstance, every challenge he faced? Or could he cleverly hide his moments of dread from his son? But no, he did not conceal or pretend. His physical strength and stature were matched by strength of character. He trusted his own judgment and was determined to let it carry him forward, regardless of any consequence.

His response to being part of a small weak tribe was to be a big strong man who never flinched, never let his course of action be guided by fear, the first impulse of Jews under oppression.

As a small boy, I played with my father's shoe on the floor of my parents' bedroom. I imagined the brown shoe was a boat I drove around the lake as I pushed it across the broadloom making putt-putt sounds. It was so big I could practically climb inside it. He wore size 15 and could only buy his shoes in specialty shops or order them made-to-measure.

This was my sense of my father, a figure of exaggerated size. He was six foot three, two hundred and twenty pounds, broad across the shoulders, a giant of his time.

And I was small for my age, a little child awed by the presence and legendary past of this big man.

In his youth, he was a champion athlete, a water polo player on the Montreal YMHA team (H for Hebrew) that won the men's Canadian title for seven straight years. Later in life, he succeeded at several business ventures and failed at others. His credo was based on strong values of family, education, religion and ideals based on ethics of Judaism and democratic socialism.

He was something of a misfit, a Jew in a Christian society, a socialist in a capitalist world, a man yearning to transform into someone else, as many men wish to do. He wore dark business suits and lived much of his life behind a desk, but there was always a physicality trying to break loose, an earthy male scent under his clothes, rippling folded arms ready to flash into action like big springs.

This sense of physical potency was unleashed in his youth, when he trained every day in the pool and became the centre and star player on the best water polo team in the country. He lived with his family of eight in a rough mixed neighbourhood, where Jews were often everyone else's favourite victims. But he refused to take on the centuries-old role of cowering, persecuted Jew and if challenged, would stand his ground and fight.

On a warm spring day, Abe and a friend were playing tennis at a public court. The two young men looked out of place volleying the ball in their whites in the east-end neighbourhood, but Abe believed if you played a game you must play it well, and that included dress and equipment. A small crowd of kids leaned against the fence, heckling and catcalling in French. Abe and his friend paid no attention. Then a ball bounced over the fence. One of the street kids, a boy of about ten, rushed over and grabbed the white ball and they all ran off laughing. Abe dropped his racquet and gave chase. He caught up to the boy half a block away and grabbed him by the arm.

"*Donne moi,*" he commanded.

The kid was obstinate, leaning the arm with the ball away from his captor.

Abe spun him around, grabbed the other arm and shook the ball loose. He picked it up and walked away, leaving the kid bawling and sputtering. The boy was joined by his friends and they all disappeared down the street.

Abe returned to the court, wiping his brow.

"Maybe we should quit," his friend suggested.

"Let's finish the set," Abe said and went back to his side to serve.

Ten minutes later, a crowd of young toughs appeared on the street. They marched toward the tennis court, arms loose, every step a threat.

"*Qui a battu mon p'tit frère?*" Who beat up my little brother, demanded the burliest guy as he burst through the door of the wire fence.

Abe hopped the net and joined his friend, whose side of the court backed onto a brick wall. They spied some loose gravel and picked up one egg-sized stone for each fist and stood side by side, backs to the wall.

The young men descended on them, led by the older brother. "*Toi!*" You! the man accused, pointing at Abe. The crowd of kids appeared at the fence and let out a cheer—"*Oui!*" That's him! The lead man rushed forward, fists first, his friends behind him. Abe blocked a punch and then connected with a series of blows with his weighted fists. The man went down. Abe fended off two others, then took on a man embroiled in a standoff with his friend, grabbing him from behind and throwing him aside. Within minutes, the entire posse was subdued. They all left, cursing and finger-pointing, a few bleeding from nose or mouth. Abe and his friend collected their racquets and balls and left the court.

That night, Abe's mother Annie, serving bean and barley soup to her youngest son, asked him how he got the nasty scrapes on his knuckle. "At the tennis court, Ma," he said, picking up his spoon.

She may have suspected the real story. Another time, she witnessed his fury at an offender in her own home. The family lived in a second-storey flat, and they were often in conflict with the landlord, who tried to bully his tenants by cutting corners or demanding extra payment. The landlord's enforcer was his thick-necked son, who always showed up when the women were home alone. Just his pounding on the door was enough to frighten many housewives into submission, especially if they came from the old country, where a sharp rap on the door often signalled violence.

One day, Abe came home from work early, walking up the flight of wooden stairs to his family's flat. As he neared the top, he heard shouting from inside his home. He bounded the last few steps and burst through the door, just catching the angry words from a male voice: "You'll do what I say!" Abe's blood rose to his cheeks when he saw the scene before him. The landlord's son had his mother Annie backed against a table, his arm raised in a threatening gesture.

Abe rushed between them. "What's going on here?" He didn't wait for an answer. He grabbed the landlord's son by the lapels, dragging him to the still-open door. The man tried to fight back, his arms flailing, losing his cap to the floor. Abe turned on his heels and in one motion shoved him out onto the staircase. The man rolled down the stairs like a rag doll, tumbling over and over in a series of terrifying bumps and screams. He landed with one last thud and collapsed in a heap. Abe peered down the staircase as the landlord's son struggled to his feet and half-gasped, half-shouted, "You'll pay for this!" Abe threw the man's cap down after him and slammed the door.

These stories of Dad's battles taught me his values of family and his choice of fight over flight in any confrontation. To this day, I can feel his strong love for his mother, who raised six children with her husband Sam, who was as mercurial as his son. No one would threaten her, not in his presence. She was a wise, patient woman who wore her white hair in a bun. She died when I was six, and all I have of her is vague memory and a single picture taken on the porch of our country home with my sister and me.

Dad learned his street-fighting skills and bravado from his father Sam, the family patriarch who died five years before I was born. Samuel David *(Shmuel Dovid)* Tafler was a strong, muscular man, not tall like my father, but barrel-chested and steel-willed. He worked in the Angus rail shops as foreman of a Canadian Pacific crew, building the wooden passenger coaches to carry immigrants to their new homes across the young country. He lost that job in 1908 when he sided with the working men in a bitter strike.

Sam was a deserter from the czar's army when he immigrated to Canada from Russia near the turn of the century. He refused to serve in the army of a country that denied him basic rights like owning land. This was in stark contrast to my mother's father Louis, who meekly responded to the draft and served his time. As the story goes, Sam had to get past an armed guard to escape from his military base in the middle of the night. He attacked the guard and left him unconscious or worse, stole a horse and fled. He kept going until he reached the nearest port and booked passage on the next ship to the New World.

On the streets of east-end Montreal, Sam mixed English with French for several months before realizing they were two separate languages. The various ethnic groups of the city formed gangs that roamed the east end and attacked each other on the streets. There were no rules to these battles, and blood and even bodies were left on the ground. One time, Sam found himself on the losing end of a fight, his neck entwined in a tightening death grip. He managed to turn his head toward his attacker and grip his ear in his teeth. He bit hard and the man released him in a howl, spurting blood. Sam leaped to his feet and spit out the ear. The fight was over.

Abe and his father before him were modern North American Jews, proud of their heritage and the promise of freedom and equality in this country. Many of Dad's conflicts involved overt anti-Semitism, and his fighting spirit was a sign of a new attitude among Jews in the mid-twentieth century, manifest on the streets of Jerusalem and in the Warsaw ghetto in 1943, when Jewish partisans took up arms to fight against their Nazi oppressors. Abe believed in pre-emption, the first punch, and was the aggressor in some of his battles. And as the tennis ball story shows, he would even manhandle a child. I admired his strength, his courage, his violence—even as I feared it would be used on me.

★

In my small lime-green office at the back of my house, the walls are decorated with scenes of the natural world of British Columbia. I have reached middle age now and I'm living in Victoria, a block from the big, black Pacific and three thousand miles from Montreal. Like my father and grandfathers before me, I live far from the place of my birth in the last half of life.

My desk is a flotsam of pens, paper and notebooks. At the back of the desk sits a dusty green velvet ring case. I open it and withdraw a gold ring, worn smooth with use. With a magnifying glass, I examine the engraving on the face. In the centre is a series of insignia laid over each other: the letter Y lies in the middle of the Star of David which rests on the old naturalist design of the Canadian maple leaf. Encircling the signet is an inscription, the letters worn on the sides: Dominion Water Polo Champions 1932–1939.

More than anything else, this ring represents my father to me. He wore it every day of his life for sixty years. I remember seeing it on his finger when he bounced me on his knee and when he sat alone and silent as an old man in a black chair fifty years later. When he died in the hospital, it went missing. We asked the nurses and the people who prepared his body for the funeral. No one had seen a gold ring. A few months later it turned up in a metal box on a shelf in his cupboard. He had taken it off because it no longer fit; his fingers had shrunk in the final months of his life.

I slip the ring on my finger. It's too big for me as well. A few times, I've tried to wear it, but it's more than the size that doesn't fit. This gold ring is my father, his accomplishment, not mine. I loved him but I also resented him, the complicated emotional mixture between many fathers and sons. It's the same with his shirts, also two sizes too big. Some I gave away to friends, others hang in my back closet.

When I look at this ring, I feel the loss of love now left to memory. The loss of a man who was the greatest influence of my life. And the loss of a chance to understand each other. The ring reflects his dual identity, the Jewish star resting on the Canadian maple leaf, like it was held in the palm of a hand. This is the split identity Abe inherited at birth, but rejected in middle life. It's an identity I still hold.

Then I think: Abe married Sarah the same year he received this award, but he never wore a wedding ring. He wore this gold sports ring instead, keeping his former identity as he gave himself in marriage.

This award reflected his pride in his life's greatest accomplishment. Or, looking back, perhaps his only great accomplishment, still more than enough for one mortal being. Abe led his team in a tough, demanding sport to defeat all other Canadian teams for seven straight years. Like men who went to war, he could never again feel the same surge of adrenaline or sense of connection with other men as he did in his battles in the pool in his younger days. War and sports hold out the prize of unequivocal victory few men can hope to achieve in any other pursuit in life.

Water polo. Men in swim briefs and bathing caps chasing their opponents around a pool fighting for a ball. Other young men played hockey or baseball. But Dad's career as an athlete was centred on the YMHA, the Young Men's Hebrew Association, and to him, the Y's main attraction was its indoor swimming pool.

The Jewish community in Montreal formed the YMHA because they weren't welcome at the YMCA. At the Jewish Y, they could get kosher food and could continue to share the Jewish experience that kept them together and separate from the rest of the city. It was a place where, behind closed doors, Jewish expression was encouraged and cultivated, not mocked or demeaned.

When Dad tried out for the team, he was a kid of nineteen, tall, gangly, but not a strong swimmer. Abe worked hard in the pool, but he couldn't keep up with the better players. The coach noticed he had long arms and good reflexes. He took him aside in the locker room.

"Kid, you want to play for the team?"

"Yeah, sure, coach."

"How'd you like to be goalie?"

"Goalie? I'm trying out for forward."

"You're not fast enough. You'll never play forward." Abe looked away.

The coach clapped him on his bare shoulder. "Look, Abe, I need a goalie. Give it a try. Practice tomorrow at six."

Tending goal wasn't the heroic role my father was

hoping to play. It was a static position at the end of the pool, usually played by the weakest swimmer. He wanted to swim, to score goals, to lead the team to victory.

It was the word "never" that got to him. The coach had erected a barrier and Dad was determined to overcome it. He had to show the coach what "never" meant to Abe Tafler.

The team practised every day for two hours after work. But Dad got to the pool twelve hours earlier, swimming lengths and throwing the ball at the net from six to eight in the morning. Then he worked all day at his job and went to evening practice with the team.

He spent a few practices in goal. Then the coach saw his swimming improve and put him on defence. Abe kept training four hours a day to the other players' two. He swam on weekends and he stayed late after practice. In a few weeks, he was swimming with speed and fluidity and throwing the ball at the net with tremendous power. The coach marvelled. Soon he was playing forward, flying around the defence, scoring goal after goal with his devastating shot. Thirty years later, I felt the stinging pain in my hands trying to block that shot in the lake at our country home, using the end of the dock as a goal.

Two weeks before the start of competitive play, the coach met him at the side of the pool.

"You've come a long way, kid." He handed him a towel.

"I've been working at it."

"You really get here at six in the morning?"

"Every day."

"It shows." The coach leaned forward. "Tell you what I'll do. I'm going to try you out at centre." This was the pivotal position on the team, reserved for the best player. Abe was expecting this, he had earned it. He aced the tryout and held that position for seven winning seasons, the top goal scorer on the top team in Canada. The best water polo player, perhaps the strongest swimmer, in the entire country for most of a decade.

In 1936, with four national championships behind them, the YMHA team from Montreal was the natural choice to represent Canada at the Olympics. But the Games were held in Berlin under the Nazi flag. Hitler's anti-Semitic campaign that led to the Holocaust was already underway; Jews were being fired from their jobs, thrown out of schools, segregated and brutalized. Under Abe's leadership, the team refused to go. My father and his team sacrificed the climax of their career and glory on the world stage to protest the darkening cloud of German anti-Semitism. I have often wondered what it would have been like for a Jewish team to have competed in Nazi Germany—or to have won a gold medal. My father, standing proud with his medal around his neck as the anthem played, Hitler and his entourage turning their backs on this team of inferiors.

The story of my father's success at water polo, a dramatic tale of triumph over adversity, became his life's defining myth. He passed it on to his family and retold it over and again, fusing with it the story of Jewish people everywhere, succeeding against the odds and the expectations of coaches, bosses, overlords and enemies. The story of an under-equipped Jewish army defeating much of the Arab world to form the state of Israel in 1948 was the paramount example of this parable of strength of will.

So my father told us that if we just tried enough, worked enough, practised enough, we would succeed. Perseverance was his watchword. "Ninety-nine per cent perspiration, one per cent inspiration"—I must have heard it ninety-nine times a year. At its best, it is a well-worn path to achievement. But at its extreme, it is the pursuit of futility against the impossible. If you find yourself banging your head against the wall, keep banging. If you keep trying regardless of the outcome, the trying itself becomes the exercise and replaces the original goal.

Determination doesn't take into account all the barriers you encounter on the path of life. And some barriers can never be overcome. The other guy may try just as hard as you, but he may be smarter, more capable or better connected. Or he may not be Jewish.

As a young man, Abe encountered barriers that were much more difficult to overcome than a dubious coach. An unofficial system of apartheid was in place across Canada to keep Jews and other minorities in their place. If you weren't white and Christian, preferably Protestant, you were second class or worse. Many jobs and professions, such as my own calling of journalism, were closed to Jews. Still in his twenties, Dad was a trucker, doing short-haul trips in Quebec and Ontario. He applied for a managerial position at Smith Transport, one of the largest trucking firms in the country. After the initial screening process, he was told he had the job. Then someone up the company ranks found out about his religion and he was passed over.

"But you don't seem Jewish," a business associate once blurted out.

"I don't take that as a compliment," Abe replied.

Born in this country, the child and grandchild of immigrants to Canada, Abe was less than a full citizen. He experienced the worst case of cold Canadian exclusion during the war, when he and others lobbied the government to accept some of the thousands of European Jews trying to escape Hitler's juggernaut. The government responded with excuses and evasions. Only after the war did my father discover that his country intentionally barred Jewish refugees who faced a death sentence. "None is too many" was the shameful motto of a senior Canadian official when considering how many Jews to rescue from the death camps.

And so, the idea of emigrating to Israel, to the only country in the world where he would be honoured instead of disgraced for being a Jew, kept circulating in the back of his head. He talked about it at family meals and kept the idea alive through his children by sending us to Hebrew school, even Hebrew-speaking summer camp, to prepare us for the big adventure of *aliyah*, the Hebrew word for migration to Israel, which means "ascending" as if to heaven.

As a child at Adath Israel school, I bought stamps shaped like leaves for five cents each to stick to branches on little paper trees. When all the spaces on a tree were filled with leaves, the money was sent to Israel to plant a real tree. Each tree was considered a blessing in a dry, desolate land, as well as a statement of redemption of the Jewish people returning to their homeland. In school and at home, we learned the Zionist creed with the Hebrew *alephbet*, and plunked coins into little blue and white collection boxes decorated with the map of Israel. Jewish pioneers dug the soil and wrestled boulders by hand. Jewish soldiers defended the homeland with bullets and blood. It was our duty to send money to support the struggle and build the nation. And so we were raised with a split identity, Canadian children who played hockey and sang "God Save the Queen" sending our allowance money with our fervent dreams to an embattled desert land five thousand miles away. But among all my schoolmates, only I came from a family that was planning to immigrate to the land of our ancestors.

And we kept the ancient laws of our forefathers, trooping off to synagogue every Saturday morning, observing the holidays and keeping kosher, following the intricate dietary laws that prohibited a list of foods and food combinations—no pork, no shellfish, no meat and dairy products consumed together at the same meal.

As a small child, my greatest fear of moving to Israel was not leaving my home and friends or living in a new country. I couldn't think that far ahead. My fear was the injections we would need for overseas travel, "needles" as we kids called them.

I remembered the visits once a year to the doctor's office for my booster shot, a blend of inoculations to ward off polio, diphtheria and other frightening diseases. I watched the balding doctor draw a large needle from a tray and, without a word, insert it into my arm. I screamed at the pain and my mother held my other arm and soothed me. For days after, my arm swelled up and ached where it had been injected.

"Do we have to get needles?" I asked my brother David about our plans for *aliyah*.

"Yeah, you especially."

"How many?"

"Five or six."

I cringed at the thought. I would rather face five or six of nearly anything than those fearful injections.

I was rescued from this ordeal as Dad's plan to move the family to Israel kept getting delayed. There was always some excuse for putting it off—the kids in school, a failing business, aging grandparents needing care. But the dream stayed alive in his mind.

★

The lake is as flat as a tabletop. It's an early summer evening in the Laurentian Mountains. The air is warm, the sun setting behind thin white clouds. The water bugs dance delicately on the surface, and a flock of ducks wing overhead to their night roosts.

My father bends his fishing rod behind him and casts his lure along the length of a sunken log, then slowly winds the handle of the reel to retrieve the line. The water is so clear I can see a large bass dart out from behind the log and attack the yellow lure. In a half-second, the fish spits it from his mouth and disappears behind the log again. Dad doesn't flinch or utter a word of disappointment, he just keeps reeling at the same slow, steady pace. Seconds later, the bass lunges at the lure again, but this time Dad leans back and pulls at the rod to set the hook in its mouth, then tugs just hard enough to prevent the fish from turning back under the log. The bass rushes and runs, leaps from the water to break free of the hook, but Dad holds firm. A few minutes later, he pulls the twelve-inch fish to the side of the boat, green on its back, white on its belly. I reach over with the hand net, scooping it under the flapping fish, then lift it into the boat.

"Great fish, Dad."

"Gave a good fight." He carefully twists the hook from the mouth and drops the fish into a metal pail. "Supper tomorrow night."

I look at the fish gasping in the bucket. It lurches tail-first, struggling for life, spiky back fin erect, eyes engorged.

Now the sun has disappeared below the horizon, the light is fading. Father and son decide to quit for the night. I step to the bow of the boat to haul in the anchor and Dad pulls on the cord to start the motor.

Memories like this are my fondest of Dad. Fishing on Fourteen Island Lake near our country home, alone together. Dad loved to fish and I acquired that love as sure as I inherited his big feet and prominent nose with a bump in the middle. Dad's nose was broken in one of his fist fights and it healed with a slight bulge below the bridge. But when I grew into adolescence and my pug nose took shape, I acquired a similar bump. It was a strange case of inherited injury. It made me wonder if I inherited all his traits, the ones acquired before birth and the others picked up through life experience.

When I was still a young boy in the mid-1950s, Dad fulfilled a promise of a trip to a wilderness fishing lodge. We drove to St. Jovite in the Laurentians, then flew north in a float plane. The plane lifted from the lake in a great wash and roar, drowning all conversation. We cruised a few hundred feet in the air, and I looked down at endless rows of fir trees covering the ground from horizon to horizon, the great Canadian wilderness spread out before me. In an hour, we landed on a lake surrounded by mountains in Parc de La Vérendrye in western Quebec.

We were deep into the backcountry and this was the only way in, no roads, no cars. We came to fish grey trout, giants of the deep that ranged to fifty pounds, nearly half the length of the boat. This was big game hunting for the sports fisherman.

We stayed in a cabin with other urban sportsmen in red suspenders, plaid shirts, hip waders. On the walls, men had traced the outlines of huge fish and wrote the dates and weights of the catch—thirty-six pounds, forty-two, forty-five. I was amazed at fish so big they were more like land animals—deer, wolves, moose. What was I in for? Could I handle these monsters?

We fished with an Indian guide, trolling and dropping lures deep to attract the big greys at the bottom of the lake. We hooked several eight and ten pounders, big compared to our bass back home, but nothing like the outlines on the wall. The next day the guide, a dark, lean man, suggested we hike to a smaller lake to catch rainbow trout. We walked over a faint trail through wilderness, and I marvelled at the guide carrying a canoe on his shoulders. We saw fresh tracks in the mud, large paws with deep claw marks. Wolf, he said. When we came to the small lake, the guide cut fir branches to make comfortable seats for us and we launched the canoe. A beaver slapped the water on the far side of the lake. We used worms to catch small rainbows, beautiful speckled fish with flashes of gold and pink stripes down their sides.

At midday we paddled back to the side of the lake to break for lunch. The guide offered us sandwiches wrapped in waxed paper, made by the cook that morning. I opened mine, white buttered bread, pink slices of meat. A ham sandwich, one of the great taboos of Jewish dietary law.

"What is it, Dad?" I asked, lifting a half-sandwich, though I knew.

"Just eat it," he said.

Abe bit into his and I did the same. I ate watching the sunlight sparkle on the lake as he chatted with the guide. So far from home, so deep in God's creation, we broke a sacred prohibition. We carried our identity with us, like the Indian guide hauling the canoe. But now we had crossed the line and eaten the forbidden food, like Adam and Eve. I chewed and swallowed each bite and wished the meat was anything else, the slippery butter anywhere else but in this sandwich, in my mouth. This was a double sin, eating the dreaded pork and mixing meat with dairy.

At home, we were strictly kosher, with six sets of dishes and silverware to accommodate different meals on different occasions. The dietary laws prescribed that the dishes as well as the food we ate must be kosher, dishes used for dairy never touched by meat and vice versa. My father was overseer of these rules. He once picked up a meat-cutting knife from the table at a dairy meal and threw it six feet into the kitchen sink. But here, out in the wilderness where no one else could see him, he let it all slide with the pink meat swallowed down his throat.

It just shows, I thought, how difficult it is to be a Jew in the non-Jewish world. They set you apart, or you set yourself apart, by dress, diet, prayer, custom. Throughout your life, time and again, you have to explain why you don't celebrate Christmas, why you're away from work on Yom Kippur, and that no, really, you didn't kill Jesus—you weren't even there at the time.

My father was stuck between the two worlds of Canadian society and Jewish tribal identity. There were times he wanted to pass as any other Canadian. Way out in the woods, he was just a sports fisherman on holiday with his son eating a ham sandwich. I sensed in my father a yearning to break free, to live his life on his own terms, rather than those prescribed by family and community. It was a desire that crystallized into a transformation many years later.

5

BUBBIE AND ZEYDIE

The old woman sat at the kitchen table, one leg resting on a stool. Chubby Checker was singing "The Twist," loud as real life. "Come on, baay-bee, let's twist again!" On the plate in front of her lay a baked potato, some raw onion, two pieces of pickled herring and a slice of rye bread leaning over the side. She slowly directed a forkful of potato from the dish to her mouth and her dark eyes met mine. Opposite her was an old man, black *yarmulke* or skullcap on his head, bent to a bowl of soup.

"Round and round and round and round we g-o-o-o-o again!" Chubby wailed. My grandmother Manya spoke, but Chubby drowned her out. I gestured at the radio and she said yes, turn it down. The music was loud to me, but the right volume to her diminished hearing.

I was in her kitchen escaping the competitive rigidity of my family, quietly slipping downstairs where my mother's parents lived in the bottom half of our duplex on Clinton Avenue. We had moved here from Wiseman when

I was seven so we could live with my aging grandparents. I turned down the radio and my grandmother filled
in with her own tune, sung softly between bites of herring and potato.

Vi bistu geveyn?	Where did you go?
Tochter meine getreye	My treasured daughter
Geveyn in Palestine	I went to Palestine
De goldene medine	The golden land
Mama, es gevesen a mechaye	Mama, it was wonderful

She punctuated the end of the song with a sigh, Oy.
She recalled a world gone by, in a dirt-floor village,
Targovitza, a *shtetl* in the Ukraine. Her own mother sang
this Yiddish folk song of the daughter returning home
from Palestine, sixty years before.

My grandmother, my bubbie, the woman who fell in
love with the third child she didn't want, was a romantic
spirit who loved to dance and sing, trapped inside a hefty
body hobbled by an abscessed leg. She had flashing eyes,
wavy black hair and an iron will that propelled her family out of Targovitza and into the New World.

In her younger years, she was a fixer, an arranger. If
you needed to get your brother into the country, she would
take the train to Ottawa, with her gimpy leg and frac-
tured English, to plead your case to the right official or
Member of Parliament. If you were a childless couple
desperate for a baby, she went south to New York with a
wad of cash and relieved a distraught unwed mother of
her newborn child. She could recite mysterious oaths and
incantations or read your future—divining a husband for
a young woman was a specialty. She used a deck of regular playing cards. Who knew from tarot?

Her obesity was a likely outcome for a woman who felt the nagging pain of hunger in her youth but now had all the food she could eat. She walked with a painful limp caused by a wound on her leg that persisted for years. In the evening, she dressed her leg in a bandage and soothed the pain with Noxzema, which she bought by the case. The sweet medicinal smell permeated the room as she spread the white cream on inflamed flesh, surrounding the oozing hole in her shin.

As my grandmother was superstitious, passionate and extroverted, my grandfather was pious, passive, reserved. It was a match made in the old country, an arranged marriage at the behest of their parents. My grandfather Louis had returned from his service in the czar's army with money in his pocket and a sewing machine, a workman's tool to earn a living. He had prospects and was deeply religious, an excellent catch to my grandmother's parents. Never mind that she barely knew him and was in love with another man, who, I found out forty years later, she had to give up to her sister due to another family arrangement. She never forgot her true love and mourned his loss when she mourned her husband after he died. If it all sounds familiar, it's the story of *Fiddler on the Roof* with a few details scrambled.

Louis and Manya had moved to a strange new country, kept a home together for more than fifty years, raised a family and nurtured grandchildren. Now, in their last years, they shared a red brick duplex with their daughter and her family. Bubbie and Zeydie lived—and slept—at a distance, not just in separate beds but in separate rooms. She likes the window open, he likes it closed, was how my mother explained it.

That day, I was there for my informal Yiddish lesson, the song of a daughter returning from the golden land of Palestine, pronounced *Palestineh*. It was a song about longing, about the separation of a mother and her treasured daughter, a common theme among the Jews of eastern Europe. Manya had left her own mother in Targovitza, and all she had of her was a picture on her bedroom wall—liquid eyes hooded by dark brows, an unsmiling face that speaks of resigned suffering.

I sat in their kitchen and listened to this exotic but familiar and comforting language passed around the table with the salt and pepper.

They taught me a few words of kitchen Yiddish— knife, bread, meat—as they worked their way through meals that often lasted two hours. A favourite expression was *keneyne hore*, no evil eye, invoked to ward off bad spirits. "You're becoming a big boy, *keneyne hore*." She couldn't celebrate the good things in life without placating the forces of evil always lurking in the background.

She also introduced me to a colourful lexicon of Yiddish invectives and insults, which were often more humorously dismissive than injurious. *Hak mir nisht keyn tshaynik*, don't bang me a kettle, is meant to silence an annoying child whose constant prattle sounded like the clanging of pots. Even more evocative was *vaks vi a tsibele mitn kop in dr'erd*, you should grow like an onion with your head in the ground. That might be said to an eight-year-old who continued to *hak der tshaynik*.

And so I began my lifelong collection of Yiddish sayings, often bittersweet invocations that implied more than they said. My favourite, supplied by my friend Yisrael, is *geshtinkiner fish g'gessin, un fun der mark oysgetriben*. The direct translation is, he ate stinking fish and was

Manya Shetzer would only agree to marry Louis if they would immigrate to the New World. She's pictured here in 1946 with a bear-like grasp on two of her grandchildren, Marion (left) and my sister Gitta. RIGHT: Manya's mother, who she left behind in Russia and never saw again.

Louis Shetzer, a pious man who made fur hats in the czar's army, spent most of his life in Canada but always dreamed of the home he left behind.

thrown out of the market. It seems like a pointless expression, but just below the surface is a complex morality tale. The man stole the fish, it turned out to be rancid, and he was caught and thrown out of the market. The moral is, if you commit a sin, you'll be punished twice: in this case, bad fish and banishment.

Another gem from Yisrael is *az got vil, shist a bezem.* If God wills, a broom can shoot. Miracles can happen, the stars can shine on the darkest night. Imagine a family of shtetl Jews hiding from enemies at the door on that dark night. If only their broom could shoot. *Az got vil.*

In the old country, Manya agreed to marry Louis on a single condition, that they immigrate to "America" to escape the poverty and oppression of the Ukraine. She was determined to raise her family in a country that offered freedom and opportunity. He went first by himself, as many immigrant men did, to find work and become established before bringing the family over. He booked passage to St. Louis, Missouri, where he had a cousin, but someone on the boat offered to buy the train portion of his ticket to the U.S. So he stayed in Montreal where the ship landed. "America is America," he shrugged. It's by such chance decisions that an entire family became Canadian, not American. At the time, Louis didn't know the difference.

Within a few months, lonely and homesick, struggling with the language, he wrote to his wife that he was coming home. She answered immediately: "Don't come back, I won't be here. I'm catching the boat to meet you." And carrying her infant son, my mother's brother Al, she left the Old World forever.

Louis was a downtrodden man with worn olive skin, thin grey hair and an unwavering dependence on his religious faith and practice. His wife called him Eli, his Jewish name. I called him Zeydie, Yiddish for Grandpa. Some of my first lessons of who we were, how we were different from everyone else, came from this man. Where Zeydie came from, a shtetl in czarist Russia, to be a Jew was to be first on everyone's victim list, living with oppression, the threat of a pogrom over every horizon. In his lifetime, he went through a remarkable transformation from hand-to-mouth poverty and wanton persecution in the old country to freedom, security and comfort in Canada. But he never overcame the mindset of the victim, the stranger far from home.

Louis was quiet and unassuming, the opposite of my father's brash, domineering nature. All these years later, I can see his bent body slowly folding into a chair, his twinkling eyes and dry, slight lip-curl of a smile. We shared a deep bond based on a natural affection that flowed between an elder and the young son of his favoured daughter. It's a bond that was set by a mutual recognition in the eyes and a young boy's empathy for an old man's suffering. In our country home, we sometimes shared a bedroom where he told me stories of the world he came from as we lay in the darkness like two brothers.

As a young man, conscripted into the czar's service, Louis was an unlikely soldier, slight, withdrawn, the epitome of millions of humble working men who suddenly find themselves in an army barracks. Skilled with needle and thread, he was assigned to the job of cutting and stitching the fur hats the Russian soldiers wore in winter. His military service was the first time he lived among non-Jews, and he avoided persecution by trading the non-kosher meat on his plate for potatoes, bread—and protection.

He prayed silently in the corner on Saturdays, kept to himself and tried to stay away from belligerent soldiers looking for someone to ridicule or harass. This mentality stayed with him throughout his life—work hard, keep a low profile and avoid those who can cause you harm.

In his eighties, he succumbed to the family weakness, vascular dementia, brought on by reduced blood flow to the brain. We called it hardening of the arteries.

When I went to see him downstairs on Clinton Avenue, he approached me and pleaded, "Take me home."

I looked at him. "You *are* home, Zeydie."

"No, this is not my home." He stared at me through thick bifocals, grimaced and sighed. "The whole weight of the world is on my shoulders." And I saw that it was and wished I could relieve it.

"Zeydie, it's okay."

He looked at me, searching for recognition. "Take me home."

I sat him down at the kitchen table. "Zeydie, where do you live? Where is your home?"

"I live . . ." His mind trailed.

"You live with us, downstairs. You live on Clinton Avenue. Nineteen hundred Clinton."

"Ninetin-hun-derd-Clinton," he repeated with his Yiddish inflection. A glimmer of memory came back.

"That's right—that's where you live."

"Yes, yes." Then in the next breath, "Take me home."

I thought for a minute. How could I assure him and ease his mind?

"Okay, Zeydie, I'll take you home."

"Yes?"

"Yes. Right now. Put on your coat, let's go."

I helped him into his heavy grey overcoat, his hat and gloves. The act of motion, of going somewhere, enlivened him. The two of us left the house and walked slowly half a block up the street, then turned around and came back. We lived on the corner and the street sign was in front of the house.

"Look, you see that sign?" Clinton Avenue. He looked at it. Then we turned to the brick house with blue shutters and twin maples on the lawn. We turned up the walk. "Now look at the number, the address. Here we are, nineteen hundred Clinton. That's where you live."

"Yes, that's where I live." His eyes brightened as we started to climb the stairs.

Inside, I took off his coat. He shuffled down the hallway and we sat at the kitchen table. He looked at me, and gradually the gloom gathered in his face again. "Take me home."

Louis lived his life longing for home. Home was the hardscrabble shtetl where he was born, wiped out by the war and the Holocaust and Soviet bulldozers. Targovitza. A place of poverty, oppression and fear. They lived on dirt floors. Marauding bands could arrive at any time to burn, to loot, to kill. A ghetto, a distant place set apart for Jews by czarist decree, because they were unfit to live anywhere else.

Long before I was born, Zeydie got a letter from Russia telling him of the fate of his parents. In the midst of a pogrom, his mother was trapped in the family store, mocked and beaten, a bag of flour dumped on her head. The place was set on fire with her trapped inside. His father went mad with grief and horror. To such a place, Zeydie wanted to go home. The family, the tight weave of culture, religion, tradition, the familiar sights and sounds and smells, the sacred blessing on the Sabbath eve—all gone, lost, destroyed, but still alive in his mind.

He grappled with ghosts in his house. I once found him talking to an open closet. "Who are you?" he asked the ties and coats. I walked over, and he turned the question on me: "Who are you?" I tried to calm him. "I'm your grandson." He looked at me with blank, filmy eyes through oily glasses. "What do you want?"

My mother tried to keep him busy, giving him long strips of cloth to fold, my grandmother's bandages for her bad leg. Handling the material reminded him of his days in the clothing trade. He folded each strip carefully in a roll and then Sarah turned around, flapped it open and gave it back to him. Busy-busy, keep working. He folded clean laundry, tablecloths, shirts, working at the dining-room table facing a wall with a large mirror.

He remembered when men would line up for jobs at the factory every day and some were sent home. There was always the danger you would be replaced—by a friend of the boss, or by someone who showed up earlier than you. One day he told me, gesturing at his reflection in the mirror in the dining room: "No matter how early I get to work, he's always here before me." My mother wanted to cover the mirror to ease his anguish, but my grandmother wouldn't allow it. In a Jewish home, mirrors are covered when someone dies so relatives will forget their own appearance and concentrate on mourning. Covering the mirrors would be inviting death into the home.

★

At fourteen, I returned home from summer camp and was shocked to see my grandfather. He was emaciated, bones tight against the skin. He had stopped talking, retreated to mumbling, groaning. I slumped into my bedroom and cried. My mother opened the door to comfort me. "Zeydie isn't well."

A week later, in the middle of the night, I was roused from my bed by noise at the front door. I looked out the window and saw ambulance attendants wheeling a stretcher to the curb. As they eased the old man into the wagon, I strained to make out his face. It was Zeydie, at peace.

My grandfather's stories of another world taught me about the balance between maintaining our identity and fitting into the larger culture. If this was difficult for me, it was much more difficult for him, in the old country as well as in Canada.

But more than anything, Zeydie taught me the concepts of home and heart. He was born and raised in a small Ukrainian shtetl called Targovitza, near Kiev, where he grew up in a Yiddish world that now exists only in memory. He died in a big city in a new country thousands of miles away, always dreaming of the homeland he left behind.

6

THE TRIBE

On a Friday night after dinner, our living room was filled with family, my father's older brother and three sisters and their spouses. "What's wrong with you?" my father shouted. The person under attack on the other side of the room was my Uncle Sam Kantor, a prosperous car dealer with a brown moustache. "How can you say these things?" Sam shouted back.

They were arguing about, of all things, the assassination of John F. Kennedy, the U.S. president shot dead in his motorcade in Dallas that very day in November 1963. My father, a bone-core socialist, was condemning Kennedy as an imperialist who tried to invade Castro's Cuba. Uncle Sam was enraged that anyone could criticize his beloved hero on the day he was gunned down. "What are you talking about?" Uncle Sam parried. The sparks flew between them like a pair of welding torches.

My Uncle Abe Socaransky, on the couch across from Sam, drew on a long cigar and blew a stream of smoke to the ceiling. He had thinning curly strands of black hair combed over his balding head and he wore a hand-tailored immaculate dark striped suit, the mark of his trade. He was telling the story of a poker game held in a flat on the Main thirty years earlier.

"And then we figured, how'd the guy get three aces again?"

I was sitting between two uncles, the three of us listening to the poker story, ignoring the battle between Dad and Uncle Sam. Uncle Abe pulled the cigar from his mouth with a flourish.

"So when this guy went to the bathroom I said, he must be cheating."

I caught my breath to suppress choking on cigar smoke.

"It turns out Harry saw him slip a card on his lap."

"Socialism!" Uncle Sam waved a finger. "Look what happened in Russia."

"Don't you know the difference between communism and socialism?" my father snapped back.

"So we watch this guy," Uncle Abe continued. "Then the next hand we grab him, and sure enough he has an ace between his legs." He paused and his audience broke into smiles.

"So we take his pants off and we put him out on the fire escape and lock the door." He waved his cigar at the window in memory of the fire escape.

"We go back to playing poker. It's the middle of winter, below zero, and he's out there freezing on the fire escape."

My two uncles have heard the story a dozen times, but for me it's a first. We all laughed out loud.

Members of the family, all smiles here, would argue and shout, then make peace in an instant. Abe and Sarah at far right and Abe's siblings and in-laws at an engagement party for my cousin Joan at Ruby Foo's cocktail bar, Montreal, 1951.

"He's at the window, tapping on the glass, begging to be let in. But we ignore him."

Uncle Sam: "Kennedy was the greatest president since Roosevelt."

Dad: "Huh! Just another American war-monger."

My mother appeared from the kitchen and called everyone to the dining room for refreshments. The stories, the argument, were dropped in an instant as we gathered around the table. She poured tea from her silver service and Aunt Helen sliced into a sugar-dusted coffee cake. "Just a little piece," Aunt Bea said.

This was a Friday night ritual my father and his family practised for thirty years in honour of his mother, who gathered the family together herself every Friday night, the beginning of Shabbes, the Sabbath. The ritual was passed on from Dad's mother to her children. This family was as tight as bolts on a ship, but they had a peculiar way of expressing their affection: through conflict. My father would argue till the veins stood out on his brow with any of his three sisters, his brother, his in-laws, his closest friends. They would shout, wave their arms, hurl insults like bolts of lightning. A few minutes later it was all forgotten as they sat down at the table or kissed good night.

Some people might find it peculiar for family members who love one another to argue so rigorously. Others say Jews are born to conflict as a defence mechanism. We are word warriors, as if the verbal struggle can make up for all the life-and-death struggles lost over the centuries. We are the heirs of the Talmudic tradition, the notion that any religious or personal issue can be examined from every angle like a diamond with a hundred facets held up to the light.

The Friday night ritual was only the most regular contact among family members. There were Passover Seders, birthdays, weddings, holidays, any excuse for a family get-together, usually enlivened by a family row.

Beyond the conflict, these people shared great love and common cause and counted on one another for comfort and support. They patronized the family businesses and helped out in time of need with unquestioned loyalty. Many of the goods and services we required were provided by various uncles and cousins, as if each planned their trade according to the needs of the family.

Uncle Abe Socaransky was the second husband of Aunt Bea, the middle sister in my father's family. His business was Cooper Clothing, a menswear factory on

St. Lawrence, the commercial byway that divided Montreal on an east-west axis, where the wares of a dozen ethnic cultures were on sale in storefronts and on the street. I went with my father to buy my first suit at Cooper Clothing when I was still a boy. We followed Uncle Abe through the corridors of the second-storey factory, past men cutting bolts of cloth with large scissors or pressing pants on giant hot irons that exhaled billows of steam.

Uncle Abe walked with measured steps over the polished wooden floors of his factory. He had a natural air of authority and a smooth gravelly patter that evoked a sense of confidence. "Come with me. We'll pick out the material." He led us through narrow rows of hanging suits and Canadian Forces jackets to bolts of cloth piled on shelves. He stopped at one aisle, bent to retrieve a dark grey bolt, unrolled a yard and rubbed the silky cloth between his fingers. "This is what they're wearing." We examined several other rolls of material, but none drew the same response from Uncle Abe.

He summoned an assistant, waved his cigar in my direction and told him to take my measurements. I stood still but twitched as the man reached between my testicles and right leg with his tape measure.

Uncle Abe brushed a fly-sized cigar ash from his lapel, then drifted away to take a call. I turned to my father. "I think I like the blue one."

"Uncle Abe says the grey one. He knows best." The grey one it was.

From Uncle Abe we bought suits, from Uncle Sam we bought cars, my father was insurance broker to the family. Cousin Jack Padveen was the family dentist, cousin Gilbert Rosenberg our doctor who made house calls.

Uncle Jack Sailor operated a hardware store in our neighbourhood and we wouldn't think of buying a screwdriver
anywhere else. We even had an underworld boss in the
family, Uncle Max Shapiro, who operated a glittering
casino where the city elite arrived in their Rolls-Royces.
When a businessman tried to renege on a debt owed to
another uncle, Uncle Max called the man and said, "You
don't want any trouble with me." He didn't. The debt
was paid the next day.

Sometimes the grip of the extended family felt like an
embrace, other times like a vice. Along with family din-
ners and celebrations came expectations—that you would
always be there, that you would dress and behave like a
little prince, that you would study and achieve and honour your elders. Shaming was a common method of en-
forcing family codes. I remember an aunt once offering
me a box of assorted cookies, then upbraiding me for
picking the one coated in chocolate.

The highest demand was scholastic achievement. You
could be an adorable, loving child, but if your grades fell
below expectations, you were devalued, dismissed. My
twin cousins, sons of my father's oldest sister, were ex-
ceptionally bright and studious. They finished at the top
of their class and went on to become academics, eventually presidents of McGill and Princeton. The rest of us
were measured by these standards. My father talked end-
lessly of the twins and their accomplishments and dis-
played their pictures in graduation robes on his wall,
rather than photos of his own children.

In our household, we lived under a regime of rules
and chores. Weekly attendance at synagogue services. No

television, except on weekends. Washing and drying dishes, cleaning the front porch, shovelling snow, hauling garbage cans. The standards applied with particular precision to conduct at the dinner table. No elbows up, of course. No one to leave the table until dinner is over. No soda pop, except on Friday night, and then only one glass. And a kosher diet, prepared by my mother, but according to the tastes and traditions of my father's family.

Study, prayer, school, respect, obedience, discipline. My father ran a tight army of three little conscripts, determined to turn us into solid Jewish citizens in his own image, to prepare us for the trials we would face in the world beyond his walls. To an extent, he succeeded, but not without filling a reservoir of resentment, which created a distance from his children that only expanded as we grew older.

One generation before my parents, the family lived in a shtetl, one of several thousand villages where Jews were settled in eastern Europe. In the shtetl, everyone knew everyone else and relied on one another for comfort and protection, for caring in sickness, for charity in poverty, burial in death. Many people in the shtetl were known by affectionate, descriptive nicknames that related to occupation or character. My old friend Jack Gardner's grandfather was Shalom Kishke—Shalom Sausage. He was the butcher.

The shtetl was the Jewish enclave where people banded together, fearful of the next pogrom that would bring fire, death and pillage. Only fellow Jews could be trusted.

Non-Jews harboured hatred and suspicion that could explode into violence at any time.

The shtetls are gone now, but the mentality of the village under siege survived to my parents' generation, and to some extent survives today. Jews continue to live together in community, out of a lingering need for protection and preservation of identity. In our case, as I was growing up, my father's family of five brothers and sisters and their spouses and children replaced the shtetl as the community we depended on for comfort and refuge.

These twenty-three members of the family formed an extended tribe that lived in different houses but were linked by invisible strands of kinship and reliance. In later life, as I studied early humanity, I came to see a connection between my own greater family and the rest of the human species. This connection predates the Jewish ghetto or even the stories of the Bible by thousands of years. The extended family of modern times is the descendant of the original tribe of people who lived together in rock shelters or huts made of animal skins.

Just like other animals that live in herds or flocks, humans live in tribes or clans of specific size that best provide for the needs of their members. For most of human history, ninety-nine per cent of the time we've been on earth, we lived in these tribal groups, hunting and gathering our food by day, sleeping in shelters at night. The numbers varied, but in much of the world, the basic social unit or tribe, like my extended family, was twenty to thirty people.

The entire species of humanity around the world is descended from small groups of early humans living in east Africa several hundred thousand years ago. Imagine a dark night back in those ancient times, a small tribe asleep in a cave overlooking an African plain. A hungry leopard on the prowl picks up the scent of human flesh. As the big cat enters the cave, a young man is aroused by the sound. He spots the flashing eyes in the darkness and shouts a warning. The other members of the tribe leap from their sleep, grab their clubs and rush to the entrance and the leopard runs off.

Humans sleep at different depth levels during the night, in a pattern that rises and falls from shallow half-sleep to deep slumber. The chance of one person in twenty sleeping at a shallow depth as a predator approaches is much better than one in three or four. Whether awake or asleep, a larger group is more likely than a smaller group to survive an attack by predators—be they animal or human.

A group of hunters is more likely to catch prey than one or two men hunting on their own. The same applies to child-rearing, shelter-building, food preparation—activities are accomplished more efficiently in groups that share the duties and the rewards. Men who killed a large animal would distribute the meat to other members of the tribe who had no food, knowing that they would also be rewarded in their own time of need.

The tribe is made up of people of all ages. There is natural interaction of men with other men, women with women, children with old people. Family is mother and father and children, but it's also uncles and great aunts and nieces and cousins. Members of the tribe aren't solely dependent on their spouses for emotional, physical and spiritual support, like so many men and women are today. The greater family or tribe forms a protective canopy, each member exchanging support and comfort with other members of the group.

The tribe invariably becomes Us, our group, which

usually leaves everyone else as Them. This is the double-edged blade of human relations—the comfort and affinity of the tribe, and the exclusion of others. It doesn't have to be this way, but it often is. I have come to believe that this is the greatest challenge of the human species, to overcome the tendency to separate, to exclude or persecute people outside our own group.

As a child growing up, I was surrounded by members of a basic social unit that often shared the roles of parental guidance and teaching. My father was a champion swimmer who was never patient enough to teach his own children to swim. So I learned to take my first dog-paddle strokes in the waves of Lake Champlain from my Uncle Abe Fleming, an ordinary swimmer but a patient teacher. My cousin Sondy taught me to skate on the ice outside our country house at Fourteen Island Lake, the same week she helped me decipher the riddle of long division from the living room overlooking the frozen lake. These extended family members were always part of our lives, in person or in conversation. I was raised in a small family that was nurtured and protected by the larger family around us.

People all over the world today live in tribal units—or spend much of their lives trying to find them or form them. They look for tribal identity in religion, in sports and clubs, on the Internet, or in communes that attempt to reproduce the social structure of the tribe.

The tribe I once lived in as a child has largely disappeared, due to death and relocation of family members. Over the years, I have tried to recreate the social unit I grew up in, choosing friends and relatives to play various roles within the tribe. Today, when I count the people who are closest to me, blood relatives or not, living near or far, I arrive at a number in the twenties, similar to the twenty to thirty people that made up the ancient tribe.

Nowadays, in recent historical times, we have replaced the tribe with the small nuclear family of one man, one woman and perhaps, children. In the small family, the man and woman rely on each other for the support they would have received from groups of men and women in the tribe. The circle of the modern family is just too small and limited to give its members all the physical and emotional support human beings need. These limits lead to frustration and conflict that often overwhelm the modern family. The small nuclear family appears to be failing as the primary unit in modern society. Many families are breaking apart into men and women living on their own, children shuttled back and forth between them.

We all need support and caring from people we love and trust, people of our own identity group, people of all ages. You can't get the same emotional connection with a girl of five that you get with her grandmother of sixty-five. The nuclear family is a closed unit of two generations that generally excludes others outside the small group of three or four people. After about twenty years, the nuclear family begins to shrink as children leave home. Thirty or forty years later it is gone forever.

Think of the names of your great-grandparents, just three generations past. If you're like me, you probably don't know them. The original tribe was multi-generational and continuous, with a lifespan and collective memory that endured for centuries. Abraham, Isaac and Jacob were the founders of the tribe and we remember their names four thousand years later, although we don't remember people just a few generations past.

The tribe is a living unit that survives the deaths of leaders and elders and passes on its values and identity to new generations.

Modern people live in large societies, but they are isolated in small nuclear families or live alone. Buried deep in the unconscious are psychic visions: ten men with pointed sticks running through the woods chasing an animal; the entire tribe sitting at the fire, men and women, children cradled in their arms, passing stories around the circle. For many thousands of years, human beings moved to the rhythm of the tribe, and we are not easily separated from our basic social unit. Nowadays, the loneliness, the insecurity, the sense of uncertainty that tugs at the soul may be a longing for the tribe.

7

BACK FROM THE DEAD

The smell of cigarette smoke drew me to the den at our home on Wiseman Avenue. I heard light laughter and music as I approached the room. I peeked around the doorpost and looked inside.

"Hello, little boy," said a striking brown-haired girl in a flowered dress, sitting on an upholstered chair. She may have been sixteen or twenty. In one hand she held a drink with ice, in the other, a cigarette, the filter stained red from her lipstick. On the arm of her chair sat a boy in a sweater and open-necked shirt.

Across the room on a sofa sat another girl, blonde and short-haired, partly hidden behind Joseph, the teenage boy who lived with our family in our second-storey home. His copper-red hair was combed back in a wave and slicked with oil. He raised his drink to his mouth and the ice cubes clinked as they tumbled to his lips. Joseph spotted me through half-closed eyes and smiled and said nothing.

The four young people were having a party in the den, breaking a list of my father's strict rules of household behaviour: smoking, underage drinking, necking or worse. And they were ignoring me, the child Joseph was supposed to be babysitting. Not that I minded. I was a little boy of four or five, content to play on my own or watch these young people cavort in the back room. It seemed like the height of glamour and daring, Joseph inviting his friends in to drink and carry on while the rest of the family was out for the afternoon.

Joseph was a seventeen-year-old refugee from Hungary when he arrived at our house a few years after I was born. His attitude to life was to say what people wanted to hear, but to do what he wanted to do, regardless of the consequences. Joseph was a child survivor of the Holocaust and he was making up for time lost in the war years by seizing any chance at freedom and excitement in his new home in Canada.

He didn't worry about the trail of evidence he was leaving behind. Smoking was a terrible fault in my father's eyes, and the smell of smoke was an obvious giveaway. But Joseph lived for the moment, and the moment on the couch with the blonde and the drink was pure pleasure.

In the late 1940s my parents took in Joseph and a young girl named Hedy, in response to a plea to sponsor Holocaust survivors who were most in need, orphaned children whose parents had been murdered. Many Jewish Canadian couples wanted infants or toddlers they could adopt into their families. My parents offered to take children of any age and were sent two teenagers.

Joseph was enrolled in high school, but most days he

would leave the house with his school books and roam the streets and hang out with a rough crowd. He was, understandably, grown up for a teenage boy. Most children and adolescents perished in the camps or on the run, and those who didn't die, quickly became child-adults.

For all his faults, Joseph was always kind and gentle to the children of the family. He would tousle my hair, smile at me and trade tickles and laughs. I was barely a toddler when he arrived at our house, and I mispronounced his name "Jofish." I never learned the details of his story, but perhaps he remembered other children my age who disappeared into the darkness.

Hedy's behaviour in our home was the opposite of Joseph's. Her survival tactics were trust and obedience. She was the dutiful girl who did everything she was asked to and more. While Joseph was free to attend school or seek adventure on the streets, Hedy was assigned to be my nanny and my mother's helper. She had a bright smile, a tall, thin frame and, like Joseph, gold-red hair.

She fed me, dressed me, fussed over me, tended to my every need. She loved me like her own child and I loved her. I was too young to know where she came from, but thinking back it seems she was showering me with attention in reaction to the suffering and loss she had experienced in the war. Later I learned she had lost her entire family and worked under terrible conditions in a slave labour camp.

Hedy's nightmare began just three years before I was born, in 1944, when the Nazis began transporting the Jews of Hungary to Auschwitz and the gas chambers worked overtime to kill as many as possible before the war ended. Others ended up in labour camps where many

died of overwork or disease. Of course she never spoke
of the horrors she witnessed to a little child. All I remember was a sweet and loving girl and the close bond
between us. Hedy eventually left us, married and moved
to Winnipeg.

Today, there are no pictures of Joseph in my parents'
photo collection. But there is a black and white photo of
Hedy, posed on a loveseat in the living room with me in
a sleeper and my sister holding a teddy bear. Hedy looks
tentatively off-camera as if waiting for a signal, her light
hair cascading down her neck. Her left arm reaches across
to hold me, and on the forearm you can make out the
labour camp tattoo. With a magnifier, the number comes
into focus: A-7846.

So from my earliest years, I began to know the people
who move in shadows among us, who came back from
the dead, the survivors of the industrialized genocide
perpetrated by Hitler and his henchmen. I had first-
hand evidence of the suffering of the people who escaped
Hitler's dragnet that was intended to murder every Jew
in Europe, perhaps the world.

Hedy and Joseph spoke Hungarian to each other and
although I didn't understand a word, I picked up some
of the nuance. Sometimes they argued and it appeared
Hedy was berating him and he was defending himself.
She told him to behave, not to blow his chance—and
maybe hers—with a family that had opened up its home
to them. But he'd had enough of authority and control
and wanted to spread his wings and fly on his own.

I remember my parents being upset when they found
out that Joseph had even lied about his own mother. They
discovered he wasn't really an orphan, his mother was

still alive. Joseph had called my mother "Mom," and when she found out the truth, it seemed a deception to her and a denial of his real mother. His reasoning for this pretence may have been simple or complex. Orphans were given priority by relief agencies, so his claim was his ticket to the New World. Perhaps he felt his own mother had abandoned him. In the midst of the Nazi roundups, some desperate Jewish women gave up their children to Christian families or boarding schools. Or he may have simply wanted my mother to be his "Mom," as a way to fit into this foreign family after the trauma of the war. But he never could. He never understood us and we never understood him, despite my parents' best intentions. Today some Holocaust survivors speak openly of their trauma, but back then they were expected to forget their past and quickly adapt to the new society.

Many years later, it all made sense to me. Joseph's behaviour was the code of the children of the Holocaust. You had to cheat and steal and lie to survive. Some took years to unlearn these skills after they were liberated. Others never did.

I can hardly imagine Joseph's sense of displacement at appearing at our home in Canada after emerging from his ordeal in the war and an orphanage for surviving children. A strange city where two foreign languages were spoken, my tyrannical father in charge of the family, three demanding young children and no one around connected to his past. This was yet another survival challenge for him, and he turned to the skills that served him in the war—cunning and deception.

About a year after he arrived, my parents arranged for Joseph to leave our home. He seemed grown up and independent and my parents were worried about his influence on their children. He left quickly and I remember him visiting once after, with the woman he married. After that he disappeared and faded into memory. These many years later I still feel affection for him, a long-lost older brother.

As I was growing up, I encountered other Holocaust survivors, the parents of some of my friends. Two of my classmates and best buddies were George Mittelman and Bernie Najman. George was mop-haired and mischievous, Bernie, tall, gentle and quick with a joke. Both were born in the years just after the war to parents who had come through the fire.

When we visited George in his family's walk-up apartment, it seemed his father was always there. He hung around the place in his bathrobe all day in a nervous condition, unable to work. George told me his father had been a successful leather goods manufacturer in Czechoslovakia before the war, but the Nazis destroyed everything, including his state of mind.

I remember Bernie's mother describing the mass arrest of her large extended family in Krakow, Poland. They were all shipped to the camp and gassed, but somehow she survived. Even her frail seventy-five-year-old grandfather endured the train ride in a cattle car. "Even he didn't die," was how she put it, meaning he was murdered instead of dying naturally of old age. I never heard her own story of suffering and survival. She had a warm, round face, but a disfiguring scar down the side of her cheek that made her smile look like a wince.

Bernie's father was a tall, well-built man who had

picked up French and a touch of elegance during the family's stay in Paris for a few years after the war. When he got angry or excited, his voice rose into a crescendo that sounded like, forgive me, an SS officer shouting orders. He too lost nearly his entire family in the Nazi death factories. A few remaining relatives were cherished. I remember an elderly aunt who visited occasionally and seemed to embody the collective spirit of dozens of family members, mournfully missed and remembered.

In later life, I encountered Holocaust survivors as a journalist and researched their stories in detail, interviewing them for hours, reading their memoirs.

Peter Gary was forced to work at sorting the belongings of gas chamber victims in Majdanek death camp in Poland: huge piles of ladies' coats here, eyeglasses there, baby strollers over there. He saved his life by stealing jewellery he found among the luggage to bribe his way out of the *zunder-commando*, the work crew directly involved with the machinery of death. He had heard that these forced workers were sent to the gas chambers themselves every few months to eliminate witnesses. So with diamonds and gold hidden under his clothes, he paid off a guard to reassign him to another work area.

Peter, in his eighties now, lives in a country home near Victoria with his chickens and vegetable garden and a menagerie of beloved pets—an old parrot, a llama and a cat. I have grown fond of him and I call him *feter*, Yiddish for uncle. He can be as sweet as any doting grandfather, but he's also prone to fits of anger and vengeance. If you cross him, he will banish you for life. "I click him out" is how he puts it, a switch that instantly turns a friend into an enemy.

This is how some survivors deal with their rage at the Nazis for cold-bloodedly destroying their families, their youth, the world they lived in. And at the civilized world for letting it happen. "I was never seventeen," Peter says in his frequent talks to schoolchildren. Not in any normal sense. At that age, he and his mother were marched to a pit in rural Poland and lined up to be shot with hundreds of other Jews. At the last moment, as the order to fire was called out, his mother fell on top of him to save his life. When the firing squad left, Peter and a few other survivors crawled out of the pit, shell-shocked and bloody.

The people who found him were afraid to shelter him, so they sent him to the Warsaw ghetto—he may have been the only Jew who was smuggled *into* that terrible place. He endured a three-year nightmare in the ghetto and in a series of concentration camps. Again and again he cheated death: when the Nazis cavalierly chose a friend instead of him to use as target practice, when he made it through illness and starvation, selections for the gas chambers. He was finally liberated at Bergen-Belsen on his twenty-first birthday, reduced to a skeleton, unable to stand.

Hitler's Holocaust was the ultimate degradation of Us and Them. And it stands as a warning to humanity: this is where we are headed when we go down the path that starts with racist resentments and the division of peoples into categories like good and evil, worthy and unworthy. When we distort the idea of identity with dangerous concepts like supremacy and exclusion. Anyone who has lived in the twentieth century can't pretend he doesn't know, can't disparage Jews or blacks or East Indians or Latinos without understanding he is taking the first step on the road to Auschwitz.

For all my life, I have lived among Holocaust survivors who play a particular role in Jewish life and the world community. They are among the world's most important witnesses to man's inhumanity to man. We must listen to them, study the lessons they teach us. Peter Gary appeared at schools for many years painfully telling his story to adolescents, eventually thousands of them. I went with him a few times. Many children walked away with tears in their eyes and disbelief at such cruelty. The ones who took it the hardest were often kids in trouble. And when Peter returned to his car, he cried as well.

When I was growing up, the survivors were young or middle-aged, now they are old men and women. In a decade or so, they will all be gone and the torch will be passed to us. We won't be able to tell the children that we witnessed the horrors, just that we grew up with those who did and tried to understand their pain and their bitterness.

8

US, NOT THEM

Something was shining near the edge of the grass. It was a collection of beads strung together, scattered on the ground, with a gold cross attached at the top of the chain. My friend George noticed me staring and came over.

"What is it?"

"I don't know. But it has a cross on it."

We were at St. Cyril Park a few blocks from Adath Israel school, the kids of my Grade 6 class and our sombre Hebrew teacher, Mr. Spiro. This was a class outing of twelve-year-olds at the end of exams, on one of the last days of school on a June afternoon. The weather was fine, the new leaves fluttering on the maples, the heat of the sun reflecting off the brick buildings.

A few of us had been frolicking on the playground equipment, little children again, chasing each other up and down the slide, wheeling in arcs on the swings. I'd leaned over backwards to watch the sky, then sat up and jumped off the swing feet-first, landing with a hop and a scuff. As my feet touched ground, my eye caught a glimmer in the dirt.

Three other kids joined us and we formed a circle around the rosary in the dust. This was an amulet, beads encircling a crucifix—a symbol of holiness to them and persecution to us. We had never seen one up close before and we were fascinated and repulsed. We knew it evoked powerful historic memories of a man who was killed on a cross, the blame and hatred for his murder directed at us for centuries ever since.

"What do they use it for?"

"For praying."

"How did it get here?"

"Some kid must have lost it."

"Probably a French kid."

"Maybe he'll come back for it."

I checked around to see if anyone was watching and no one was. The rest of the class was on the other side of the park with Mr. Spiro.

Throughout these few moments, no one picked up the rosary or suggested we take it. Like tribal children who know bad magic, we all understood why we shouldn't touch the small chain of cross and beads. This was their symbol and even handling it was dangerous, a threat to our religion.

And some of us knew the historical link between a Jewish person with a child's rosary and the charge known as blood libel, the accusation that Jews kidnap and murder gentile children to perform some strange ritual that involved drinking their blood. These were fables from the Dark Ages, but they were still current in some circles when I was a boy and are still current today. If a child disappeared in medieval Europe, it was common practice to blame the Jews and seek revenge. Or the local Jew-haters would invent the whole story of a missing child so they could launch an attack on the ghetto. It may seem a far stretch to transfer a bizarre myth of the Middle Ages to a playground in Canada; but this was only fifteen years after the war, when a similar psychosis led Hitler on a rampage far worse than any medieval atrocity.

Our teacher Mr. Spiro came by. A gentle, pale man with an east European accent, he was likely a survivor of the Holocaust, or his relatives were—or more likely, were not. He stood behind us for a moment, five Jewish children bent over a cross. He was the same man I once saw pick up a crust of bread left in the gutter and carefully wrap it in paper and place it in a waste bin, to avoid offending the memory of those who died of starvation.

"It's time to go," Mr. Spiro said.

We looked up at him. "Leave it," he said. "It's time to go." And we joined the rest of the class and walked back to our school.

This was Montreal, the New World, but still the old Canada divided into separate groups that kept to themselves. Like the Jews of many European countries, we knew that our existence in a Catholic milieu entailed inherited suspicion and mistrust handed down through the centuries. We didn't know what child left that rosary lying in the dirt at the playground. We didn't know if he would come back for it. But we did know we didn't want to be accused of separating him from his sacred cross.

★

School is all about rules, which children often ignore. And parents sound repetitive by the time their kids find out that other kids are more interesting and original. Where children really learn many of life's lessons and prove their worth to themselves and their peers is on the playground, especially when they're left on their own.

A few months after the time at St. Cyril, I was playing ball on a hot sunny day at Kent Park, a long rectangular field with several baseball diamonds at one end. There were half a dozen of us playing a scaled-down version of softball we called scrub, each of us batting and running and fielding every position in turn. When it was over, I was exhausted and sweating, the heat gathered in my cheeks and at the back of my neck.

I approached the drinking fountain, ball glove in hand. There was a lineup of smaller children waiting for a drink. I stood by impatiently, wiping the perspiration from my brow with my sleeve. I stared at the small trickle of cold water burbling upward as little kids slurped and swallowed.

I kept tight to the line, children milling around me. Two small girls in pigtails, sisters no doubt, were next at the fountain. They were black kids, maybe six and four, dark-brown-skinned in a sea of small white faces. The bigger of the two lifted the smaller one to the top of the concrete base to drink from the spout. Then she put down her sister and drank as well. Behind them stood a little white girl in pink overalls, about the same age. She stared at the two sisters, wide-eyed and confused. "You're so . . . so dark," she said. "What happened to you?" She seemed totally innocent, astonished to see children with dark skin. I took a quick drink and looked up. The two sisters turned and left.

I wanted to tell that girl in pink overalls, "It's nothing, they're like you and me, just a different colour." But I didn't. It seemed so futile, so impossible. The little girl wasn't expressing hatred, just childish surprise. She was young and uninhibited and could express her true feelings.

I've thought about that incident at Kent Park for years. That's how easily differences arise, feelings are hurt, little children are humiliated. I felt guilty that I was too embarrassed to say or do anything. Maybe it was the duty of the little girl's parents to prepare her to meet people different from her. But not everything can be taught. Some things have to be learned—or unlearned—through experience. I suspect if the little girl in pink had been a few years younger, she never would have noticed the difference.

This was the old Canada, where nearly everyone had one thing in common: white skin. There were a few black railway porters and Chinese laundrymen and Indians tucked away on reserves, but the entire grand assembly of humanity most everywhere was white. A person with dark skin stood out. Many people were raised in Canada without ever seeing one.

I also thought about how this moment at the drinking fountain would affect the two sisters. Maybe they were already accustomed to being treated like a curiosity. If not, they would be soon. Throughout their lives they would have to face the unspoken reflection of their difference on the faces of white people they would meet. People who stretched out their hands and said, "Pleased to meet you," while their eyes mirrored their thoughts, "Hmm, black, I wonder where she came from."

★

Kent Park was where my friends and I usually played softball and we considered it to be our field. It was on the edge of a growing black community that had moved up from the Little Burgundy area near downtown. One Sunday afternoon, we gathered at the park, throwing and fielding balls to warm up. Soon a group of black kids began arriving at the same diamond.

I was batting grounders when a muscular black guy in a sleeveless T-shirt took the ground next to me and started hitting balls as well. Now there were twenty-odd players in the field jostling for balls. The black kids were much noisier and more flamboyant than we were, running in front of each other to chase balls, jumping and whirling in the air as they threw to each other.

"Hey, Charlie, c'mon—hit it!"

"Let's go, let's go!"

"First base! Comin' home!"

"Double play, man."

Soon we all retired to the side of the backstop, two sets of teams intending to play on the same field.

The kid with the sleeveless T-shirt stood behind home plate. He still held the wooden bat in his hand, twirling it.

"What you guys doing here?" He faced us and rested the bat on his shoulder.

"We're playing a game," said Allan, stepping forward. He was tall and athletic, one of our leaders. "We were here first."

A smaller black kid walked up to him. "This is our field, man."

"It's a city field. We were here before you."

Players from both sides picked up their equipment and started tossing balls and pounding their gloves. It was a standoff and neither side was ready to give in.

"Look, let's settle it," said Stanley, a wiry blond kid, one of my close friends. "We'll flip a coin. Winner takes the field."

We all gathered around. Stanley produced a quarter from his pocket and said to the guy with the bat, "Call it." He flipped the coin in the air and the black kid called, "Tails!" The silver coin landed on a slanting angle in the grass, the queen facing up.

"Okay, guys, let's go," said Allan, putting on his glove.

"Hold on," said the muscle-kid with the bat. He stood in Allan's way, lowered his head and stared at him. "You heard what he said. This is our fucken field."

"We won the toss," Allan said, his glove on his hip.

"Fuck it," said the muscle-kid and he waved the bat at Allan, then stepped up to home plate and pounded it. His friends followed him and took the field.

We retreated behind the backstop. Some of us cursed and complained, and we left to find another field, vowing to throw off any smaller kids who were playing there.

Claiming a ball field by arriving first was an old unwritten rule in the parks. But they considered this field their turf, and that took priority over old rules. To us, a coin toss seemed a fair way to settle the difference. To them, it was just another white man's trick to push them aside. Nothing superseded their right to territory, the place where they always played. They were prepared to split heads to uphold that right. We weren't prepared to have our heads split.

An adult often thinks he has the solution to a child's dispute, even decades later. Now I am that adult thinking, why couldn't we have all played together? Our side against theirs, or even two teams picked from both sides. But this adult wasn't there. And the young boy who was, answers back, "It wouldn't work. We came to play with us, not them."

9

THE HOUSE ON THE LAKE

A hail of rocks flew from the bushes, landing all around us, one striking my arm. A small pack of boys rushed to the road, each holding an arsenal of stones in his hand. There were two of us and five of them.

The biggest boy named Darcy led the pack, slick black hair and flashing eyes. He blocked our way.

"You can't go here!" he shouted.

The rocks flew. My friend and I dodged and swerved.

"Go home! You can't pass here!"

We tried to stand our ground. "It's a public road!"

"Not for you!"

Soon the rocks were depleted and we got close enough to the five boys to talk rather than shout.

"We're not letting you pass," said Darcy.

"Why not?"

"This is our territory."

It was as simple as that, another primeval, territorial

conflict, carried out with stones and bodies, the first human weapons. We were just a short walk from our country home in the Laurentian Mountains, a sprawling old house with a back porch that overlooked Fourteen Island Lake, *Lac des Quatorze Iles.*

To me, this place was a childhood paradise where I played with my friends and explored the hilly woods and the lake, free of the drudgery of school and homework— but not the tribalism of the city. Even here we had our little enclaves of English, French and Jews, engaged in their games of rivalry and exclusion.

We got caught up in these games just by walking to the corner store a mile from our home to buy candy. My usual companion on these trips was my buddy Victor, which we shortened to Vicky before we knew it was a girl's name. He was one of six children of a German-Jewish furrier named Fritz Nobel.

Vicky and I would stroll past familiar homes for the first stretch of the walk, waving to people we knew, our Jewish neighbours. Soon we would leave friendly territory and begin passing the homes of strangers. The fear would rise in my chest as we approached the sharp corner in the road that followed a rocky point in the lake. Between the road and the water, partly hidden by trees, was a large house that commanded the point, the Clark place. Here we'd walk single file, watching the woods at the side of the road, hoping to pass unnoticed. But this day, they were waiting for us with stones, hiding in the bushes.

"You can't stop us," Vicky said. "The road isn't your territory."

"Yes it is." They stood in our way, blocking our path.

We tried to outwait them, standing on the road with arms crossed. But they weren't giving in.

They started picking up more rocks, murmuring to each other in menacing tones. Maybe we would try again later, climb through the woods beside the road to get around them. But right now, we weren't going to make it to the candy store.

One of them stepped forward, a small sandy-haired kid. "Why don't you go back to Israel?" he taunted. Israel, a place we had never been, not for two thousand years. We hardly knew where it was.

Instead we went back to our homes, where we played with our own kind—and sometimes abused and terrorized our younger friends as these kids abused us. Call it what you like: imitation, displacement or childish cruelty.

Of course, children learn these lessons from their parents, who play these games at a more subtle level. At one end of the lake was an exclusive private club, where members played tennis in their whites and sipped gin and tonics. Exclusive meant gentiles only. Well, so what? We could have lots of fun at the lake without their stuffy club. Except they had motorboat races at the club. Different race classes for different horsepower motors, with buoys marking the course; races for adults, races for kids, prizes for the winners. Speed and water, roaring engines, glamour and glory. We yearned to compete in their races, but all we could do was watch from a distance. No boat races for the wrong race. One Jewish kid I knew managed to get his boat entered by asking a non-Jewish kid to drive it in the race. He wanted to show that his Jewish boat was good enough, or even better than the Christian boats. This was the mid-1950s, about the same time a black woman in Alabama named Rosa Parks refused to give up her seat on the bus to a white person. She helped start a civil rights revolution in the U.S. and people in Canada cheered her bravery. We needed a Rosa Parks to lead young boys on the road to the candy store.

One day in midsummer we were just finishing lunch when I heard someone call from the front porch. I went to the door and saw a woman with red cheeks and shoulder-length black hair peering through the haze of the screen window. It was Mrs. Clark, mother of the little Cains who attacked us with stones. She wore loose-fitting shorts and blouse, the standard woman's attire of the summer cottage dweller.

"Hello," she said with a weak smile. "Is your mother home?" She looked past me in the direction of the kitchen where Mom was putting dishes in the sink.

Sarah opened the door to greet Mrs. Clark but she did not invite her in. The three of us stood at the edge of the porch, beneath the branches of the great oak that spread above our yard.

"How are you, Mrs. Tafler?" Now the smile grew wider.

I wondered what this visit was about, but for the first few minutes Mrs. Clark would only talk about the lake, the weather, the children. I could smell a faint whiff of alcohol. Perhaps she had needed a drink as fortification for this chat with the Jewish woman. Gradually, she began to steer the conversation to its point, the country club and its policy of exclusion.

"You see, Mrs. Tafler, things are changing at the club."

Mrs. Clark drew a cigarette from a pack, struck a match and lit up and kept shaking the match after the flame was extinguished. She held the cigarette delicately between her fingers.

"We had a long, drawn-out battle last weekend." She leaned forward as if to take Sarah into her confidence. "You wouldn't believe the things that were said. But I stood up—it was my motion—and we managed to get it through."

"We are going to allow"—she took a breath—"you people to join. On a trial basis.

"It was a tough fight. You know, these feelings, they go way back, they're deep in the bone. Some people will never let go. I wanted no exclusion—period. They amended my motion to a one-year trial. We'll vote on it again next summer. But it passed with a clear majority."

My mother couldn't find the words.

"So now it's up to me, as the one who put it through, to get the word out." She looked past us at the door. Perhaps she envisaged a chair or wanted to use the bathroom. She wouldn't ask and my mother wouldn't offer.

"Let me extend the invitation, to you and Mr. Tafler, to join the club. You can be the first. Fifty per cent reduction on fees, the summer's half over."

"Well . . ." My mother looked back at the house.

"Do you play tennis? We have lovely courts. And the motorboat races are on next week." She glanced at me. "Your boys can enter."

"I'll have to ask my husband."

"Of course." She exhaled smoke with a sigh. "And how is Mr. Tafler?"

"He's fine." Now Sarah offered a weak smile. "He'll be here on the weekend."

"Wonderful!" Mrs. Clark clapped a hand on her thigh. "You can drop by the club."

My mother looked doubtful.

"Or just call me if you have any questions."

We had no phone at our country place, but Sarah didn't tell her that.

"Nice to see you, Mrs. Clark."

"And so nice to see you." She took a last puff and stubbed her cigarette butt into the ground. She walked to the end of the path, then smiled and waved and went on her way.

Of course we didn't join the club on the far side of the lake. The wound of years of rejection couldn't be healed that quickly. But for years, I wondered why the policy of exclusion was changed. Maybe some of the old haters had gone to their just reward. Or maybe the club needed an infusion of fresh money—of course the Jews have plenty of that. Or perhaps Mrs. Clark represented a changing Canadian society, a gradual discarding of old ideas of excluding people because of their religion or race. She may have been awkward, but she did show courage, at the club and at our place. In keeping with Canadian custom, the change was one tentative step at a time, starting with a trial membership at reduced rates. But the country club on Fourteen Island Lake may have been a small sign of the gradual shedding of the old snakeskin of Canadian apartheid.

"I got them," my friend Bobbity whispered, though there was no one else around.

"What?"

"Smokes."

"Let me see."

He walked to the side of the road and stretched open the pocket of his shorts to offer a glimpse of a pack of Sweet Caporals, his mother's brand.

"Wow!"

"We're going to meet Vicky up in the woods and smoke them. C'mon."

Lawrence Hibbert was a rough kid, with dark tousled hair and a wild streak of rebellion. His adoptive mother called him Bobbity, a nickname she borrowed from a ditty in Walt Disney's *Cinderella*, "Bibbity-bobbity-boo!" Bobbity was my only gentile friend, his country home next to ours surrounded by Jewish families. He was a year older than me, and much bigger and stronger. As an antidote to his child-like nickname, we further nicked it to "Bob."

We all suspected Bobbity was abused, long before we ever heard the term. It's something kids can spot at fifty paces, the hangdog look of a child, the severe, pinch-faced demeanour of his parent. His mother, something of a *Cinderella* character herself, called him from a distance in her shrill voice: "Bobbity! *Bob*bity!" He would run home, and you could hear him pleading and sobbing before the door slammed behind him.

Bobbity dressed better than the rest of us, sometimes in starched white shorts and shirts with collars, as if Mrs. Hibbert was trying to prove something to someone, perhaps the adoption agency. Or it could have been an impossible challenge to him to come home clean after playing in the woods. I always wondered about parents who were picky about cleanliness, who allowed their children to run free in the outdoors and expected them to come back clean as a fresh napkin.

Bobbity was a playful but unpredictable boy, prone

to wanton misbehaviour and angry, violent outbursts. I admired him, I suppose because he was older, but also because he was exotic and dangerous.

I wasn't sure I wanted to smoke my first cigarette that summer day, but I couldn't resist following Bobbity up into the woods. Smoking was one of my father's strictest taboos, based on addiction and damage to health. After a ten-minute hike up the hill, we found Vicky sitting on a log in a small clearing. Bobbity opened the pack and handed out smokes all around. We used several matches to light up.

I inhaled gingerly, and an exotic, musty taste filled my mouth. I choked, went dizzy and coughed the smoke out of my lungs. The three of us strutted around the clearing, waving our cigarettes, acting like tough guys in a movie. The sunlight streamed through the canopy above us, dappling the forest floor. In the far distance, a woodpecker drummed on a tree trunk. We began laying branches around the perimeter of the clearing to mark it as our territory.

Bobbity lit a second smoke from the butt of the first one. I looked at him, flicking an ash from my cigarette. He was self-assured for his age, a child trying to escape childhood. He was sturdier, more physical than us Jewish kids. He spoke differently, with a flat English-Canadian tone, without the hint of an Old World Jewish inflection.

We both had strict parents—his mother and my father —but he took chances, careless of the odds against him, while I was cautious. When I broke the rules, I always looked for an alibi, an escape route, a believable excuse. In half an hour, I'd be back home and my mother would never know about this transgression by her precious little boy. But Mrs. Hibbert would notice the missing pack of Sweet Caporals. She'd smell his clothes and his breath for confirmation. And she'd demand a confession and then punish him all the worse if he lied. Bobbity didn't just fail to cover his tracks, he left a clear trail behind him. But he didn't care, or he couldn't help himself. At the age of nine, he was already recklessly oblivious to the consequences of his behaviour.

To Abe's three kids, the place on the lake was a wilderness playground. We were free to roam the woods and discover nature, to fish and swim, catch frogs and minnows, play hide-and-seek with our friends. But to him, it was responsibility, bills, repairs, mixed with the occasional break—diving deep into the water on a summer's evening, casting for bass with his youngest son. But mostly it was work. While his kids were jumping off the neighbour's raft, waterlogged and howling with laughter, Dad worked on the house with hammer and wrench. It was an old country home with a floor that ran crooked past the chimney upstairs where I slept and felt the warmth of the hearth on my shoulder.

Dad hired workmen for major jobs like installing the furnace, but he did most of the maintenance work himself—plumbing, carpentry, general repairs. Mom wanted a knotty pine interior. Dad spent most of a spring, summer and fall ripping out cheap wallboard and installing lovely, blond pine panelling throughout the main floor. The house was his proud accomplishment, his gift to his wife and children. I realized it was his choice to repair while we played, to leave the office behind and work with his hands. He loved the sense of accomplishment of a finished job he could see with his eyes and feel with his fingers. At the front of his house, over the entrance, he nailed up a sign, which he had hand-painted: Gan Eiden, Hebrew for Garden of Eden. The sign was a mark of our heritage and the love he and his family shared for this place, their little paradise.

But in the Garden of Eden you know there's a snake, and you know he will cast us out. The house on the lake stood empty for long stretches, vulnerable to intruders. One day in the fall, Abe and Sarah drove up by themselves. A neighbour must have called them. When they opened the door to their country home, water oozed out onto their feet. Someone had broken into the house, plugged the kitchen sink, opened the taps and spread detergent everywhere. There was an inch of soapy water on the wooden floors throughout the house.

When people break into a country home, they invariably do it for one reason, to steal anything they can lay their hands on. But this was a simple act of vandalism. Nothing was taken. The floors were ruined, our family's sense of security in their home in the woods was violated.

Who would do such a thing? Sarah and Abe had no known enemies in the area, they got along with everyone. Abe was the kind of man who would give away an antique chair to a neighbour because she said it once belonged to her grandfather. When my parents were mopping the floors, they found something peculiar in the living room: a silver rubber knife, a child's toy. The moment I saw it, I recognized it. It belonged to my friend Bobbity.

Why would Bobbity break into our house to vandalize the place? I remembered an incident from the previous summer when I was visiting his home next door. We had just returned from a romp at the lakeside and our shoes and legs were streaked with mud. Mrs. Hibbert, one of her Sweet Caporals trailing smoke, joined our conversation.

Suddenly she turned to me. "How often do you have a bath?"

"Once a week," I told her.

"No wonder you people are so dirty."

I felt an emptiness in the pit of my stomach. I tried to explain we bathed in the lake, often three times a day, but she wouldn't listen. Later I realized her words cut so deeply because they were intended for Bobbity as much as they were for me. We were buddies, bonded by children's games and secret rituals like smoking in the woods. Now she was telling him I was an unsuitable playmate, not clean enough for his company. And that my family and my people were also unclean. I tried to ignore and forget, as children do. I wanted to maintain my friendship with Bobbity.

I started to put the pieces together when my parents told me of the flooding and the rubber knife. My father had reprimanded Bobbity for some misbehaviour a few months before. And then there was his mother's strict, abusive child-rearing and her comment about our family next door.

Bobbity, as children are, was a reflection of his mother. Sometimes the mirror is cracked or distorted. Sometimes a child will try everything not to be like his parents, but that too is a reflection of his upbringing, the life lessons he learned at the breast, the cradle, or the strap. Some evil seed was planted inside him that sprouted and grew from stolen cigarettes to break and enter and wanton destruction. Bobbity must have asked his mother, and she must have told him, why she thought the neighbours next door were "dirty people." Other people use clubs or fire, but Bobbity attacked with soap, to cleanse us. He was too young to know that the dirt his mother spoke of was in her own mind, and too confused to know that his pain and fear couldn't be eased by flooding the neighbours' house.

No child was ever born to hate. To suckle, to gurgle, to laugh, to cry. But never to hate. Every child, every family of children, every generation, has to be taught one by one, that the people who are different are not to be trusted. Generations of infants are born without the knowledge that Jews are evil, blacks are stupid, Indians lazy, Chinese devious. They must be taught, with great sense of purpose, one at a time.

My father had the floors repaired, but he couldn't repair the stain in his heart. He never told me, but I suspected that this was the final affront that sealed his decision a few years later to give up his life in Canada and move to Israel. Other than friends and family, there was nothing more precious to him than his home in the country. That a child could attack this place, that the culture he was raised in could somehow encourage this act, was intolerable to a man who had struggled all his life to achieve his rightful place in Canadian society.

PART TWO

MAN

10

LEAVING CANADA

In the garage Dad was packing. Under a hanging lamp, he filled wooden boxes with possessions he and my mother had collected in thirty years of marriage. He worked with purpose and concentration, as he always did, taking their lives apart piece by piece. He disassembled my mother's crystal chandelier, wrapped it in newspaper and stuffed it into a wooden box. In other boxes went antique serving platters, a set of silverware from Birks, his art collection—paintings of horses and ducks and Canadian winter scenes of country roads and houses. He carefully wrapped a fabulous carving of three Inuit building a kayak, thirty pounds of polished jade-green soapstone. Surely he would be the only person in Israel with one of those.

"Where did you get the boxes, Dad?" There were twenty of them, finely crafted, each the shape of a small coffin.

"They came from Russia, someone shipping over scientific instruments. I bought them from the supplier."

From Russia to Canada to Israel, just like our family. He kept packing, didn't break his concentration.

I stepped closer to catch his eye.

"You know it's hard on Mom."

"Your mother will be fine." And he closed the lid and sealed the box with packing tape.

Hard on my mother, and hard on me as well, although I didn't tell him that. It was 1970 and I was a young man, trying to separate my life from my parents, conflicted by my sadness at my mother moving halfway across the world.

At fifty-six, my father was finally fulfilling his dream of moving to Israel, a plan that had been percolating at the back of his mind for most of his life. He and my mother were packing up or selling their possessions to make the move to Kfar Menachem, a kibbutz south of Tel Aviv. Most North American Jews were content to take the obligatory organized tour of Israel, visit Jerusalem where they pressed a wish scribbled on folded paper in the cracks of the Western Wall of the Temple, and fly back home. My father was one of the very few who planned for the day when he would leave his comfortable life in Canada and fulfill his Zionist dream. Abe experienced anti-Semitism first-hand in his formative years, and he knew of the waves of oppression Jews had endured throughout history. He was convinced that Israel was where he belonged, that Jews outside the homeland would always walk a knife's edge between tolerance and persecution.

But now my mother was reluctant. Moving to Israel meant giving up her intimate circle of family and friends. She had three young adult children she loved dearly and grandchildren on the way. My brother had married and launched his career in journalism in Montreal, and my sister was studying medicine in Toronto. Sarah had nurtured her ties to family over a lifetime, and the prospect of missing the birth and early years of her grandchildren was particularly heartbreaking.

Loyalty to the family tribe had been a constant value of my parents' lives together. How could they just give it all up?

Abe and Sarah would leave behind their comfortable three-bedroom home in Canada and move to a small apartment on the kibbutz. He promised her trips back to Montreal every two years, and their three children agreed to visit them in Israel in the alternate years. And he vowed he would move back to Canada if she ever wanted to return. But it was an empty promise. The strength of his character and commitment would never allow him to turn back.

I went upstairs, where my mother fumbled through tablecloths and crystal glasses. What could she take, what wouldn't fit in their new home? Abe plowed through personal papers and old letters and stuffed them in garbage bags. He had no trouble casting off superfluous items, giving them away, throwing them out.

Who wants a dining room set?

You like that painting? Take it.

In her kitchen, my mother fretted. "He just throws things away. It means nothing to him. How can he just leave everything?"

To the casual observer, Abe lived a good life in Canada, a country admired by millions of people around the world, including many who would give anything to live here. He had a rich family life in Montreal, and the adversity

he faced was minor compared to the persecution Jews
were subjected to in eastern Europe. But he never felt at
home in this country, knowing he was seen as an outsider, the Other, by many Canadians.

Canada is a peaceful, prosperous, expansive nation,
with hardly a battle on its soil in its 140-year history.
Israel is a small, overcrowded country surrounded by
enemies, always in a state of military alert, and frequently
at war. In Canada Abe was a successful insurance broker
who owned a duplex in Montreal and a five-bedroom
country home in the Laurentians. In Israel, he lived in a
small flat, struggled to learn a new language and worked
in a cowshed, ankle-deep in manure in ninety-degree heat.
And perhaps most ironic, in Canada he was an observ-
ant Jew who kept a kosher home and prayed in the synagogue every Saturday. On Kfar Menachem, a secular,
socialist community, there was no rabbi, no synagogue,
no religious practice of any kind.

Abe's relatives, especially Bea and Helen, two of his
three sisters he had been close to all his life, were ap-
palled at the idea of my parents immigrating to Israel in
their fifties. To give up their home, business, family, all
their contacts, was beyond reason.

Shortly after he arrived, Abe wrote an article in the
kibbutz newsletter: "We came to the conclusion that,
essentially, life of North American Jewry is no different
from that of eastern Europe or any other exile." Montreal equals the Warsaw ghetto. It seems far-fetched, but
not in his mind.

The cowshed where Abe worked in his first years on
the kibbutz was a small, mucky feedlot for raising beef
cattle. For many people this would be a miserable place

to work, but Abe was living the dream. Besides fulfilling his life's goal of living in Israel, he was tending cattle. Some men find their passion at the golf course or in the garden. Dad loved cows. Back at home, his favourite TV program was *Rawhide*, a show about a cattle drive starring Clint Eastwood. He watched it every week but was only mildly interested in the story line about the cowboys' latest entanglements. He liked to watch the herd of cattle rolling across the plain raising a great cloud of dust. "The cows are the best part," he would say as the credits scrolled by at the end.

On the TV version of the American West it looks like fun, but raising beef cattle in Israel was a challenge. Feed for the animals was scarce and the dry climate provided no pasture, which severely limited the size of the herds. But Abe didn't come to the kibbutz just to raise cattle, he came to solve problems, to contribute new ideas. He brought his take-charge attitude with him, despite his rudimentary grasp of Hebrew and his superficial knowledge of the delicate science of raising cattle in a hot, dry country.

In Canada, he had heard of a new process of converting chicken manure into cow feed. He took a quick course in animal husbandry at Macdonald College west of Montreal and gathered all the information he could about this exotic new feeding method. Kfar Menachem had half a million chickens, the largest poultry farm in the Middle East. Eureka—the solution to the problem of cattle feed lay right under their noses in the chicken coops.

Feed chicken shit to cows? *Ma atah omer?* What are you talking about? The kibbutzniks thought this big man from Canada had stood too long in the sun. But he was willing to raise the money to run a test on a small herd, so they went along with his scheme. Dad solicited funds from friends in Montreal to buy the machine that gathered the chicken manure and processed it into cattle feed. The big red machine that looked like a grain harvester was shipped to Israel and put to use in the chicken coops. And the converted manure was fed to the cattle.

As the animals bent to their new feed, a skeptical kibbutznik turned to my father. "Are they really eating it?"

"They are."

"Yes, but do they like it?"

Like it or not, the cows kept eating and most important, gaining weight. Word of this new system spread across Israel, and Abe became a minor celebrity in his adopted land. The next year he won the Kaplan Prize, awarded annually by the Israeli government for innovation and efficiency. Kibbutz members were amazed—this man comes from Canada, never worked on a farm in his life, and he shows us how to raise our cattle.

Yes, he showed them how. And perhaps they resented him for it. Years later, on a visit with my parents in Israel, I saw the red machine rusting on the side of a road. Now in his sixties, Abe had left the cowshed for less physically demanding work, managing the kibbutz general store. And the chicken shit to cow-feed scheme was abandoned and never mentioned again. Perhaps it turned out to be impractical or even dangerous as a potential transmitter of disease to humans.

Abe moved on with vigour and enthusiasm to remodel the general store, where members bought everything from condoms to chocolate bars. Any disappointment he may have suffered in leaving his cattle was washed away by the sweat of his brow. In his Montreal milieu, men earned their living and stature pushing papers around desks in office buildings. On the kibbutz, physical labour and the fruits it produced were highly esteemed. The new Jews had to prove to themselves that they could build the country with their own hands, coax the crops to feed the nation out of the hard-baked soil. Abe loved to work his body, and he wanted to contribute to this communal society in the embattled Jewish state. Whether he was chucking manure in the feedlot or hauling boxes of pop in the store didn't really matter. Perhaps best of all, he had his darling bride to himself, instead of having to share her with thirty family members.

Sarah became the coordinator of the young volunteers who came from around the world to work on the kibbutz. She made the best of her new life—trips to Jerusalem, the Sinai desert, adventurous mountain hikes with sturdy kibbutzniks. But she mourned the absence of her family. Another birthday, another Passover, the birth of a grandson celebrated with handwritten letters instead of hugs and kisses.

But her loyalty to her husband overcame all else. She was often asked—out of his earshot—how she could agree to give up so much and move so far away from her home. The response was always the same. "I couldn't say no to him. It was his dream."

After work hours, my parents retreated to their three-room home. They spent many of their evenings reading, listening to music, watching television in English, the BBC news or piped-in American programming.

For all their devotion to Israel and their eagerness to fit in to the kibbutz, Abe and Sarah were middle-class urban Canadians, set apart from kibbutz veterans who were raised in the shtetls of eastern Europe and had lived on the collective farm for forty years. Israel is a Middle Eastern country, in mindset as well as geography, largely populated by Jews from Arab countries. The way of life, based on survival in a tiny struggling country surrounded by enemies, is a far cry from the gefilte fish gentility of Jewish existence in Canada. Everything from the war-planes screaming overhead on manoeuvres, to the spicy Moroccan food and the chaotic rush to board the bus is unsettling to North Americans.

The Hebrew language can be a maze of confusion to an English speaker, and Sarah particularly struggled with the rapid-fire speech Israelis blurt out like machine gun rounds. She was confounded to learn that words that sounded like English have different meanings in Hebrew: *he* means she, *who* means he, and *me* is who. Gendering is another complication—every noun is either masculine or feminine, and every verb is spoken differently as it refers to a man or a woman. And Hebrew writing is like hieroglyphics to newcomers. The letters are written back-wards from right to left, without vowels or capital let-ters, and bear no resemblance to the English alphabet.

Sarah retreated to her books, written in English by American and Canadian authors. Robertson Davies was her favourite. She still baked coffee cake, cherry pie and other North American desserts, still dressed in fashions from fine Montreal shops on Friday nights, instead of the shapeless cotton shifts the other kibbutz women wore.

Abe and Sarah were committed converts to kibbutz life, but they couldn't leave behind their urban Canadian identity. Sometimes on my visits I would catch veteran kibbutzniks staring at my mother. Her hair was just too well-groomed, her skin too radiant for an elderly kibbutz woman. And she wore the diamond ring her husband gave her on their engagement. No one else on the kibbutz had such a thing. When Sarah became engaged in Montreal in 1939, these people were breaking dry ground by hand and eating bread and beans and half an egg a week.

In Canada they were Jews, but in Israel they were Canadians. Surely Israel is a country of immigrants, but the newest arrivals to any place often seem the strangest. Besides her great loneliness for family, my mother missed the details she remembered of life in Canada. "I wish I could hear a crow call," she told me when I visited, and I imitated the cawing sound. "I wish I could feel the snow on my face, just one more time."

11

DO YOU HAVE A GUN?

Late at night I was awakened by a blast of gunfire. I opened my eyes and caught the faint light at the window. The English girl I was sleeping with rustled beside me.

"That sounded close," I said, just above a whisper.

"Not too close," she murmured.

I wondered who was shooting, our side or theirs, who was running in the dark, who was dying.

A few hours before, we had heard firing in the distance as we made love under the blankets. Now the gunshots were closer. We had met the week before, both of us working in the kitchen at Kibbutz Malkiya. She was blonde and sweet and nineteen, a couple of years younger than me.

The firing kept repeating sporadically as we lay in the single bed by the window.

"What do you think?" I asked, not sure what I meant. She rolled over. "I think we have to get up in a few hours."

Oh yes. The pots will be waiting for me in the kitchen. Pots that were used to cook mounds of vegetables, soup, stews. Pots so big you could practically climb into them to scrub the rings of brown grease and bits of gristle stuck to their sides.

I rolled over and pulled a pillow over my head to muffle the noise. And I gradually went back to sleep amid the sound of a small war being waged somewhere outside my window.

Malkiya was an isolated settlement on the Lebanese border in northern Israel. The main crop on the farm was peaches, which grew in an orchard that ended at a barbed wire fence marking the border.

I had decided to try out kibbutz life shortly after my parents moved to Israel. After travelling thousands of miles across the world to be with them, I moved eighty miles to the north to establish my independence. I was a young man just out of university with no particular life plan. I had graduated from Sir George Williams in Montreal with a degree in sociology—in other words, no employable skills. After fifteen years in school I wanted to get out of the classroom to experience the world. Picking peaches and washing pots on a kibbutz was as good an experience as any, and it appealed to my Zionist inclination to live in Israel, as part of a majority ethnic group for the first time in my life.

I worked on the kibbutz with fifteen other young volunteers from Europe, North America, Japan. At 5 a.m. the fruit pickers would be driven to the orchard in an armoured vehicle. Sometimes on the hill across the fence, we would see Arab farmers in white *khaffiyas* leading their donkeys and tending their fields. The Lebanese farmers were not hostile to Israel, but the Palestinian fighters who lived among them were engaged in ongoing guerrilla raids and skirmishes.

In Israel, the idea is, the border begins where people live. If there's nothing but miles of empty space between the boundary line and the first community, you could lose that land to invaders. So the imperative is to build settlements on the border in the most difficult and dangerous parts of the country. For volunteers, young foreign travellers in the 1970s, living in this outpost in the mountains was an adventure, and an extension of the ongoing countercultural movement that was sweeping the Western world.

We picked fruit before breakfast in emerging dawn to avoid the hottest part of the day. The tree-ripened peaches were the sweetest fruit I have ever tasted, the syrupy liquid spilling into your mouth as you bit into the flesh.

Attached to the kibbutz was an army base, the soldiers assigned to protect the settlement and the paved road that snaked along the border. The road was subject to sporadic terrorist attack; a school bus had been blown up killing a dozen children a few weeks before I arrived.

The guerrillas would try to sneak over the border, cutting the barbed wire and setting off bombs or hijacking cars on the road. Or sometimes they just shot across the border from the hills. The Israelis would shell guerrilla positions with artillery or launch raids into Lebanon to destroy Palestinian bases.

One summer evening I watched two young mothers pushing strollers in the fading sunlight. They stopped by a building and admired each other's babies in the long shadows cast by the nearby trees. As they chatted, I noticed the wall behind them was dented with shell holes the size of fists. This was the attitude of the kibbutzniks to the ongoing attacks, a mixture of defiance and indifference.

The soldiers from the base patrolled the kibbutz and accompanied us to the orchard. I got to know one tall Israeli soldier my age. He showed me his Uzi submachine gun, the clip, the firing mechanism.

"Is it a good gun?" I asked, holding it in my hands.

"Yes, it kills well."

I spent my first weeks on the kibbutz in the midst of a rainy January, lonely for friends and family. My only comfort was a bottle of Canadian Club I had purchased at the airport, which I emptied one miserable night in my drafty bunk. Soon, spring emerged and I began forming friendships with other young volunteers and grew accustomed to the pace and rhythm of kibbutz life.

Despite the low-grade war all around us, I don't remember fear as part of the experience. It was easy to downplay being in the line of fire because so many other people, such as the soldiers in the nearby base, were in greater danger. After a while the gunfire became so much background noise, like random fireworks set off by neighbourhood kids.

Perhaps the greatest danger was travelling on the road to the kibbutz. It weaved beside the border along some desolate patches where guerrillas could easily slip over the barbed wire or shoot a rocket at a passing vehicle. One time my parents came to visit me by car. Along the way, they picked up an Israeli soldier who was hitchhiking. "Is the road dangerous?" my father asked. "Oh no," he replied. Then he added, "Do you have a gun?"

Once you get used to the sound of gunfire, you begin

to dwell on the ordinary elements of life. Like, who will I sleep with tonight? And the next morning, what's for breakfast? After three hours of picking peaches, we would eat it all—cucumber and tomato salad, boiled eggs and omelettes, baskets of buttered rolls, thick, rich cream and yogurt. I was the only volunteer who spoke Hebrew, so I became the interpreter and middleman between the foreigners and kibbutzniks. The most important issue to mediate was work, what jobs the volunteers would do, which varied from kitchen duty to sorting peaches in the packing plant.

A week after I arrived, I lobbied to get out of pot-patrol in the kitchen and became a peach picker and part-time English teacher to the students in the high school. The kids were infatuated with Western music, especially the Beatles. I played the Sergeant Pepper album in class and wrote out the lyrics on the blackboard.

"What about Lucy? Why is she in the sky with diamonds?" asked a bright-eyed girl in the front row.

"It's just a song."

"Is it about drugs?"

"No. It's about a girl with diamonds."

The last English teacher had been dismissed from the kibbutz for taking drugs. I smoked Lebanese hash in my cabin with the other volunteers out of sight of the Israelis, who thought it was a degenerate habit associated with Arab culture.

My friends were these volunteers, young men and women from all around the world. There was Tony from Spain, Hans from Holland, Masaki from Japan, Richard from New York, brothers Rolf and Hans from Germany. And the English girl and her bunkmates from Paris and

California. We formed a kind of distant satellite of Haight-Ashbury, indulging in drugs, sex and '60s music, high in the mountains between the Israeli Army and the Palestine Liberation Organization. I was a Jewish youth from Canada, a committed Zionist who spoke passable Hebrew, but my peer group was other foreigners, mostly non-Jewish young people of the countercultural movement, not the Israeli Jews all around me.

The Israeli men my age were tough and battle-hardened, many of them veterans of the 1967 Six Day War between Israel and the surrounding Arab states. To train for warfare, they struggled up and down sand dunes in their army boots carrying forty-pound packs. They told me of combat at close quarters, turning a corner and seeing an Egyptian soldier an arm-length away and shooting him dead. One man even showed me forbidden photos of the victims, bodies in uniform trailing blood in the sand. They thought of me as soft and coddled, an American kid in shorts and T-shirt who barely knew a gun from a broom. The young Israeli women, many of them trim and beautiful, also served in the army but in non-combat roles. They wore uniforms and were as tough as the men and just as dismissive of a wandering Jew from Canada trying to find himself in their country.

Service in the armed forces was the rite of passage for all Israelis. Another young man, an immigrant to Israel, told me in Hebrew: "Go serve in the army. That will make you an Israeli." I thought of boot camp, battle and blood. Not for me.

After three months in Israel, my tourist visa expired and I went to the immigration office in Tel Aviv to get it renewed. A man behind a desk wearing an open-necked white shirt checked my papers and asked a few questions.

"*Atah Yehudi?*" he said, looking up from my passport. "Are you a Jew?"

"*Keyn.*"

He stamped a one-year visitor's visa on an inside page.

I walked out into the blinding midday sun feeling light-headed. His question would be considered hostile anywhere but in this country. This was the only place in the world where being a Jew was an advantage.

I was a Zionist at heart, convinced of the moral imperative that led the Jews back to their homeland. I loved the boundless energy and enthusiasm of the people, the sense of building the future rather than just letting it unfold, the varied landscape from rocky desert hills to citrus groves that bloomed fragrant white flowers in the late winter. In Canada, it seemed, life just drifted on and there was little common purpose or sense of identity. In Israel, the survival of the nation was at stake, and the modern miracle of a country reborn after two thousand years was still playing out. Every person had a role in this drama, whether they drove the Egged bus from Tel Aviv to Haifa, or led the nation from the prime minister's office in Jerusalem, or marched off in uniform to battle the enemy in the next war.

I travelled the country, from the northern border settlements to the Red Sea in the south and down to the Sinai Peninsula, where at daybreak I retraced the steps of Moses up Mount Sinai to receive the Ten Commandments. In the Old City in Jerusalem, a mélange of Orthodox Jews in black hats rushing to prayer and Arab merchants tending their souvenir shops and spice stalls,

I made my way through narrow streets to the Western Wall of the Second Temple. I trembled with awe and wonder and nearly broke down as I touched the great ancient stones of the last fragment of the Temple destroyed by the Romans two thousand years ago. I had learned about this place as a child and now here it was before me, the holiest site of Jews around the world, a place of age-old tragedy now redeemed by a modern Jewish nation.

I had a deep emotional connection to Israel, but committing my life to this country was another matter. The language, the culture, the climate, were not entirely foreign, but they were not mine either. These people were fellow Jews, but I was a Canadian and they were Israeli, a distance apart. And this was a difficult place, of war, heat, dense population.

There was deep irony at play in my decision of whether to stay in Israel or return to Canada. For nearly two thousand years, Jews have yearned to go back to their homeland and never saw the place beyond their dreams and prayers. In modern times, hundreds of thousands fled persecution and struggled to reach the ports at Haifa or Ashkelon to find refuge in the emerging state. Now, I could decide on a whim whether to stay or climb into a jet aircraft and leave.

It was my memories of the role of the outsider that tipped the balance. When I was young, the immigrant experience was seared deeply into my consciousness. In Montreal, I grew up among immigrants, people who were mocked and shunned for their accents, their strange customs and foods. To this day, I empathize with the newcomer who grapples with a new language, who misses the familiar smells and sounds of his native country, the scent of jasmine, the click of the cicadas.

I remember my grandfather whispering stories to me in the dark when I was a child. Forty years after his death, I can still see his face, remember his anguish. "Take me home," he pleaded. Where is that? I wondered. He spent most of his life in Canada, but his roots were still buried deep in the place he left behind, a place that no longer existed. From early adulthood on, he was a stranger in his adopted homeland. As a young boy hearing his stories, I vowed that would never happen to me.

12

THE INTERVIEW

I delayed my return and any decisions about restarting my life in Canada with a hitchhiking tour through Europe and North Africa. After a few months, my money running out, I caught a ride from Lisbon across the Atlantic on a Norwegian freighter as a work-away, cleaning the boilers in the engine room in return for board and passage.

In three weeks we landed in New York and I boarded the first bus to Montreal, gripped in cold winter weather. I arrived at the downtown bus station carrying my knapsack and spent my last ten dollars on a cab ride to the duplex on Clinton.

If Israel didn't feel like home, Montreal, though familiar, certainly didn't either. My grandparents had died, friends and family members were dispersed, and my parents, back in Canada to clear up some final details, were focused on their new homeland, which I had just left. I had been gone for a year and my old roles of student, son and kid playing ball with his buddies had faded away.

My immediate concern was figuring out how to find work to survive in the city. I had never held a job and had few skills beyond picking peaches. The best plan I could come up with was converting my experience teaching English to kids on Malkiya into a full-time job. I quickly prepared for the transformation from travelling vagabond to responsible teacher. I cut my hair and dug out my white shirts and business suit. After a few days of scanning the classified ads and phoning schools, I landed my first job interview.

I took the bus to an imposing ivy-clad building on the west side of the city, a residential school for delinquent boys. In the outer office, waiting to meet the principal, I was joined by another young man who was also wearing a suit and tie and overcoat. He had close-cropped brown hair and a bony, square face.

Thinking back, it seems strange that the principal would leave two job candidates together for a long ten minutes in this overheated, windowless waiting room. Maybe he wanted us to get to know each other.

I exchanged a few words with my fellow prospect and then he said, half-asking, half-telling:

"You're Jewish, aren't you?"

"Yes, I am."

"Do you think you'll get the job?"

"I don't know. Do you?"

"Could be." He smiled and cocked his head. "Why don't you think you'll get it?"

"I don't have a teaching degree."

"Neither do I. No big deal in this place."

"Really?"

"They take what they can get." He inched closer to me. "Do you think they discriminate?"

"I can't imagine." I was beginning to feel assaulted by his forwardness.

"Neither can I. No, really, I mean it. You people are clever, good at business. It would make sense to hire you."

All I could do was look at the door to the principal's office, hoping it would open.

"I mean it. If I was hiring, I'd hire Jewish people. They'd be good for my business."

I searched for the words to respond. He was trying to appear sympathetic, but he came across as intrusive and patronizing. I wondered what kind of game he was playing. Then the secretary appeared and called my name.

I walked into the principal's office and he stepped forward to shake my hand, a tall, angular man in a tweed suit.

The interview went quickly. He examined my resume and other papers, looking up frequently to catch my eye.

"No teaching degree?"

"No, sir."

"Ever worked with kids in trouble before?"

"I haven't. But I've done some teaching in Israel."

"Israel?"

"On a kibbutz. I taught English to school kids."

"I see." He looked up at me. "Do you want to look around?"

"Sure."

"Come with me." He folded the papers and stood up. As we left his office, he stopped at the doorway. "One

thing to watch out for. The boys will test you—from the
very beginning. Don't let them get away with it."

We walked through the long corridors of the school.
Young boys appeared from doorways to peer at us. He
showed me a classroom and introduced me to teachers
and staff. Then he took me upstairs to the spectators'
gallery above the gym. Down below a special event was
taking place, a school fair, with booths set up where the
boys could throw balls or rings at targets. At one booth,
a pretty teenage girl stood below a sign that read "Kisses."
The boys lined up to eagerly kiss this young girl, and
then they went back to the end of the line.

We returned to the corridor where we encountered a
veteran teacher. We stood talking, the principal, the
teacher and the job applicant—a young man in a grey
suit not much older than the students in the school. Suddenly I felt a thump at my back. I turned and saw three
boys standing behind me, a look of sour defiance on their
faces. One of them had struck me, carefully and quickly
enough that I couldn't tell which one. Like the principal
said, I was being tested. I said nothing to him or to the
boys, so I suppose I failed the test.

My interview over, I shook the principal's hand and
went back through to the outer office where the other
young man was still waiting.

"Did you get the job?"

"I don't know."

"Maybe we'll both end up working here."

I put on my overcoat. "I think there's only one job."

"But you never know." He smiled and blinked—or
did he wink?

"The best part of the job is"—he barely lowered his
voice—"you get to follow the boys into the shower."

He chuckled, but I didn't. His laughter tried to cover the comment as a joke. I wasn't sure if it was, or not. We both wanted the job, but he might have wanted something else as well. As I left, the secretary called him into the office.

A week later, I received a letter from the principal telling me he hired someone else. I never knew, but I always assumed it was other young man in the waiting room.

13

MAÎTRES CHEZ NOUS

There's thousands of people in the streets! They're throwing rocks, fighting with the cops!" I shouted into the pay phone as the scene unfolded around me.

"Get back out there," my news editor barked back. "And be here at eight to file your story."

I hung up the phone and rushed into the street, clutching my notebook and pen. Stones were flying from every direction and riot police were attacking demonstrators with three-foot batons. Suddenly someone hurled a boulder into the phone booth I had just left. It crumbled into a pile of broken glass. I had missed being part of that pile by a few seconds.

A protest march had turned violent and a five-alarm riot was raging on the streets of Old Montreal. It was a chaotic scene, sporadic battles spread over several streets and alleys. Protesters attacked police with placards or threw rocks at any convenient target. Police attacked demonstrators or anyone else at random. I smelled smoke and felt the electric sense of human fear in the air. In the distance, I heard the sickening crack of nightsticks knocking heads.

A group of rioters rushed a van with the call letters of an English-language radio station. The driver gunned the vehicle in reverse to escape. A squad of riot cops, their nightsticks swinging, attacked·the mob. The rioters dispersed as fast as dust blown off a desk, mowing down a knee-high picket fence in their path.

I ran to the brick entrance of an alley.

"Look what they did to me!" A fellow reporter named Gerry showed me the bloody gash on his head.

"I was holding up my press card"—he held his hand out as if he was warding off the devil—"and they bashed me!" Gerry wore a sheepskin coat and had shoulder-length hair. To a riot cop on the rampage, he looked like a protester.

"Watch out!" he shouted. "Here they come!" And we ran off in different directions.

Back at the newsroom, a dingy ground floor office at the Canadian Press, I worked feverishly with four other reporters and editors to piece together the night's events. I was only six months into my first job in journalism since returning from my wanderings in Europe in early 1971. I got the job with the help of my brother David, an editor at the Montreal *Gazette*, and abandoned my plan to become a teacher. Our task that night was to dispatch reports on the news wire to inform the country and the world of the latest bloody chapter of the revolution brewing on the streets of Montreal in the early 1970s.

The demonstration was organized by the labour movement to support workers involved in a bitter strike at *La*

Presse newspaper. Whatever the issue, street battles like these generally embodied the cause of *Maîtres Chez Nous*, Masters in Our Own House, the escalating battle of Quebec nationalists trying to break free of Canada.

We were writing the first draft of history, but the view on that October evening was hazy and confused. Covering a riot is like trying to count the waves in an ocean. You only see a small part of what's happening at any time, and the scene is changing by the second as your attention shifts from note-taking to running, dodging rocks and batons and, in the days before cellphones, finding a phone booth to call the office. Reports are often dominated by statistics and data supplied by police: how many demonstrators, how many injured or arrested, how much property damage.

As clearly as we could see, ten thousand demonstrators marched through the streets to the *La Presse* building, shouting and waving placards. Their path was blocked by a line of metal barriers and a cordon of police with riot sticks and helmets. The surging crowd pressed against the barriers, the police waved their batons. Then a hail of rocks flew at the police from the back of the crowd, the barriers collapsed and the street battle was on.

So who threw the rocks? Provocateurs brazen enough to start a riot, but safely out of the reach of the nightsticks themselves. Were they extremists on the fringe of the movement—or police agents who infiltrated the protesters so the cops could bust some heads? We couldn't tell. The tinder of two hundred years of class and language hostility was scattered on the streets that night. The rock throwers just supplied the spark.

"Okay, let's file the story." Darcy O'Donnell, our

sixtyish editor with thinning, curly grey hair was directing traffic in the newsroom that night. He peered over
the main writer's shoulder. "Take out that comma," he
directed, pointing at the second paragraph.

At the Canadian Press Montreal bureau, one small
satellite in the constellation of news wires around the
world, we were always big on the small points, but often
missed the big points. Our reports that night would be
short of analysis, of the story behind the story. Just the
facts, ma'am, supported by the police sources we phoned
from the newsroom, despite the presence of three of
our reporters in the midst of the riot. "160 injured in
Montreal protest" the headline reads across the top of
the yellowing newspaper I've kept all these years in a
manila envelope.

Fifty teletype machines chattered throughout the office, cigarette smoke drifted from the desks to the fluorescent light fixtures. Frank Grey, the slick, black-haired
chief writer, pulled the copy paper from his ancient black
typewriter and handed the assembled story to the
teletype operator. The operator retyped the article and
dispatched it to head office in Toronto to be distributed
to hundreds of newsrooms across Canada and around
the world.

Most newspapers have one or two copy deadlines
a few hours before the presses start rolling, but at the
Canadian Press we were supplying media in many different time zones, so our deadlines were constant and
usually three minutes from now. CP editors literally
wrote the book on news writing style—it's called *The
Canadian Press Stylebook*—and the perfection of every
word, every dash, every space between the letters, was of

great significance. More than once, I felt my entire body seize up under the intensity, as I pushed myself beyond the limit to achieve impossible levels of speed and accuracy.

The newsroom was something of a dungeon, the windowless ground floor of a dilapidated building on St. Alexander Street in lower downtown. The air was thick, the floors were grimy and strewn with paper, the raw material of the trade. The clamour of the teletype machines was so persistent that editors and writers in their fifties had all lost their hearing. Perhaps the most common word heard in the building, especially from Al McNeil the sports writer and Boris Miskew the business editor, was "Whatsat?"

The office hierarchy was a reflection of the old Lower Canadian society we conveyed to the world in our news dispatches. At the top of the pecking order was Bill Stewart, the crisp, reserved bureau chief who smoked French cigarettes and occupied the corner office. He was only involved in the Big Decisions. Bill had served as a correspondent in the Second World War, reporting on the Canadian troops' valiant battles in Italy. We cheekily called him "William of Anzio," after the Italian beach town that saw heavy fighting in the final stages of the war.

Next door was heavy-set, prickly O'Donnell, the assistant bureau chief who ran the operation, exerting authority over content, commas and hyphens. News people like to be known for their fabled stories, most involving daring exploits, usually spiked with alcohol. Darcy's legacy involved a bloody fist fight with a federal cabinet minister on the train between Ottawa and Montreal that was apparently sparked by rivalry over the minister's wife. He also recalled an episode of such staggering drunkenness that he was certain his wristwatch was running backwards: drunk at eleven, still drunk at ten. Another time he became so frustrated with a story he hurled his Underwood typewriter out a second-floor window. Of course the window was closed at the time.

Both of the senior managers in the newsroom were late-middle-aged, English-speaking men. These two generals and their Anglo lieutenants operated the main information agency transmitting the news stories of a largely French-speaking society to the outside world. I doubt they recognized the irony. This was old Quebec, where the boss invariably spoke English and the workers spoke French, the very bastion the demonstrators on the street were trying to storm.

The higher-level executives of the operation were the CP brass in Toronto, but the ultimate bosses were the handful of wealthy newspaper owners who controlled the news service, almost entirely Anglos as well. The reports we filed, ostensibly free of bias, were invariably favourable to corporate interests, the established order and Quebec remaining in its place in Canada. Bill Stewart spoke fluent French with an authentic Québécois twang and even smelled like a French bistro, chain-smoking his unfiltered Gitanes. But he took his orders from head office in Toronto, which held a patronizing, impatient attitude toward Quebec, Canada's over-emotional Latin Quarter.

The CP newsroom was neatly sectioned in half by a room divider, French reporters on one side, English on the other, noses buried deep in typewriter keys, and little communication across the divide. We worked in both languages, and the English writers were careful to clean up the clunky quotes of French Canadians we interviewed in English.

So, "De goddamn cop do de fight, you know dat," became "The police started the fight," Mr. Laberge said.

We operated twenty-four hours a day, but other than nine-to-five office hours the front door was locked. The primitive method used to gain access to the building was to ring the bell to summon Angelo, the short Greek janitor who wore dirty green overalls and smelled of cleaning solvent. Angelo appeared to inhabit the building day and night. Whenever we rang, we seemed to awaken him and he would stumble to the door dishevelled and foul-tempered.

"Open the door, Angelo," we shouted from the entrance.

"Fuck-a-you!" he yelled back.

Angelo was at the bottom of the hierarchy performing the menial jobs, like thousands of other immigrants in Quebec. He hauled mounds of waste paper out of the office, stuffed into a huge garbage bag he dragged along the floor. He spoke hardly any English or French and he reminded me of the Hunchback of Notre Dame, grunting and bearing his load.

As a young man with a passion for journalism, I loved the work, revelled in the excitement and discounted the downside. This was much better than teaching a roomful of bored, unruly kids. I rented a small furnished apartment on Durocher, just a few blocks from the newsroom on St. Alexander. I was in my early twenties, at the centre of the most exciting city in the country. I had money in my pocket and access to a hundred bars and discos, where young men and women chased each other like tropical fish in a tank seven nights a week.

In the newsroom—we loved the term and other lingo that set us apart from ordinary office work—I was accepted as any other struggling young journalist. As the Jewish kid, I was given the ethnically relevant assignments: Israeli Foreign Minister Abba Eban, visiting Montreal, invites the Egyptians to face-to-face peace talks. In Russia, the Soviets discover ancient Hebrew manuscripts and allow copies to be shipped to Canada for study by Jewish scholars.

I could fit in as long as I could keep up the feverish pace and exacting levels of accuracy, and match my colleagues elbow to elbow at the nearby tavern, the Bar des Arts, or at the press club in the old Sheraton Mount Royal hotel, where we sometimes drank till dawn, then staggered off to a house party.

We were handmaidens of the system, the news industry that sold the party line to the masses, but we got to see our names in print and we had front-row seats at the historic events of the day. The most important were the grinding trials of the October Crisis, the 1970 drama in which a British diplomat and a French-Canadian politician were kidnapped, the politician murdered. We reported every legal manoeuvre in detail, shining an accusatory spotlight into the eyes of the men charged with fomenting revolution in the name of Quebec independence.

The new society of French-speaking Québécois was struggling to be born, to replace the Old Quebec dominated by *les Anglais*, a battle waged on the streets and in the courts and the legislature. In the office of the

Canadian Press, we were telling the story, but we also *were* the story. But like the man who sees the trees but not the forest, we were barely conscious of our own reflection in the mirror we presented to the world.

When I tell people I'm from Montreal, they invariably say, what a wonderful city. Sometimes they add how they'd love to live there. Would they? Would I? Montreal is the most vibrant, colourful city in Canada. For me, it's a place of personal history, friends, relations, familiar old places. We all tell our own life stories, with ourselves at the centre of events hopefully in sympathetic roles.

I choose to remember my leaving Montreal as an adventurous act of self-determination. I was off to explore the world and discover a different kind of life. I never liked winter, the cold, the ice, the driving snow. I wanted to live in a smaller place, closer to the wilderness, free from family constraints. I was never fully comfortable in French and found working in both languages difficult.

And, I was invited, if not told, to leave. Along with hundreds of thousands of other English Quebecers, many of Jewish origin, I was told specifically, your future is elsewhere. The road to Ontario is that way. You may speak French, but you're one of them. *Les autres*. It doesn't matter how long your family has been here, you never will be one of us. *Jamais*.

This message was conveyed a thousand times, through people on the street, the media, the government, the laws they passed diminishing the English language and the English minority.

Even my friends told me. One night I was drinking beer with a French-Canadian colleague at a bohemian bar downtown called the Seven Steps, the kind of place we went to every other night. We both smoked cigarettes and drank a few and a few more. In vino veritas. Soon we were arguing over French-Canadian nationalism, the debate of the day.

"Can't you see? Quebec should be its own nation." He blew smoke at me.

"Why? Quebec is strong inside Canada."

"Quebec will disappear inside Canada."

"How can you say that? Québécois culture is stronger now than it ever was."

"What do you know about it?"

"What do I know? I was born here."

"Yes, but you're not French."

"I speak French," I sputtered. "I know as much about it as you." The words rang hollow in my mouth. Here we were in Quebec's major city, speaking in English as we argued about French.

He fixed me with a half-drunken stare: "You don't belong here."

"What do you mean?" I put down my beer on the table between us.

"Why are you here? You don't belong here."

I thought for a moment and found I was unable to disagree. The rise of Quebec nationalism had made me feel like an outsider in my own home.

The further irony was, he wasn't even from Quebec, he was from Ontario. But he was francophone and I was, well, anglophone and Jewish—two strikes and you're out. It's hard enough to be a minority, but a minority within a minority in 1970s Quebec felt like I was unwelcome in both languages.

In the fall of 1973, I quit my job at Canadian Press and left Montreal with my future wife Jen to spend the winter in Mexico. We had met in Montreal a few months before, fell in love and decided to travel together. We drove my Chevy Vega station wagon across Canada, down the west coast of the U.S. and into Mexico. I knew this was more than just an adventure, an extended holiday, it was a move away from the place of my birth.

Life is full of swings of the pendulum. French Canadians felt they were threatened and had to protect their culture or they would gradually disappear. I agree with them, and I think the world and particularly Canada would be impoverished without the French language and Québécois culture. But to assert themselves, they had to threaten other cultures, including my own, which is sensitive to threats, real or imagined. English was seen as the enemy that had to be suppressed if French was to survive and thrive. We Jews were seen as English, because we spoke it, even though the English never really accepted us. So the French enacted laws that promoted their own language and suppressed English, restricting its use on storefront signs and in the workplace.

A few hundred thousand people ended up in exile, an unfortunate by-product of the goal of strengthening Quebec culture. Was this inevitable? Does your gain always have to be my loss? No one was forced out of Quebec at gunpoint. But people of my background have learned to read the signs and pack our bags before the guns are pointed. At nationalist rallies, thousands of people gathered in the streets, waving the blue and white flags and chanting Le Québec aux Québécois. Clearly that didn't include me, even though I was a native son, my grandparents' and great-grandparents' bones buried in Quebec soil.

Many of us left, including all my immediate family,

my brother and sister relocating to Toronto. But hundreds of thousands of other English Quebecers, Jews and non-Jews, stayed behind. And they thrive side by side. In my old neighbourhood, Orthodox Jews wearing black hats walk past Québécois professors with rimless glasses and leather briefcases. They may not be good friends, but they don't scowl at each other.

I enjoy visiting Quebec as much as anyone who wasn't born there. Like my father, I was a loyal son. I had a deep love of French culture, the streets and alleys and forests of my childhood. I just wish I hadn't been thrown out, in the rare moments when I admit that I was.

14

EVERYMAN IN CALGARY

The door burst open and a reporter in a rumpled sports jacket rushed to the phone at his desk. He dialled his office, opened his notebook and began dictating his report for the noon news: "At city hall, council is still debating the budget." Actually, they weren't. Ten minutes earlier, the debate had ended and council had approved the city's budget.

I was sitting at the next desk in the Calgary city hall press room. The radio reporter had arrived from the bar and called in his report without bothering to check the council chamber. I had a choice to make. Say nothing and leave him out to dry. Or tell him his report was wrong so he could fix it.

"Ralph."

"Yeah?" He was bleary-eyed, his hair falling in bangs over his brow.

"They just passed the budget."

"They did?"

"Have a look." Ralph rushed through the door that led to the council chamber. A moment later he came back. He picked up the phone and called quickly. "Hold that report, they passed the budget."

In the spring of 1974, Jen and I returned to Canada from Mexico, gravitating to Calgary where we stayed with my old buddy Harvey from Montreal and his girlfriend Shelby. I landed a job as a reporter at the *Calgary Herald*, the city's main newspaper, and Jen as a nurse at the Foothills Hospital.

In the mid-1970s, Calgary was in the midst of an oil boom fuelled by the latest crisis in the Middle East. The city was remaking itself and growing in all directions to accommodate the influx of new people. The big money was flowing to the oil companies but a healthy side stream poured into the building industry.

At city hall, we journalists were the self-appointed watchdogs of the gatekeepers who approved plans for new suburbs and office towers worth hundreds of millions of dollars.

Calgary was a city of brash, eat-what-you-kill capitalists. It was also a place of open prairie friendliness, rooted on the farms and ranches where neighbour depended on neighbour, even if they lived miles apart and only saw each other every few months.

In Alberta, it was what you could do that mattered, not where you were born or who your parents were. On the prairie and in the oil patch, the hierarchies were still being formed and there was much more fluidity among the ruling classes than there was in the east. This was a city in the making, the financial centre of an upstart, renegade province creating its destiny and flexing its muscles within Canada.

Only in Alberta could a short, stout, heavy-drinking reporter named Ralph Klein become mayor of Calgary and then premier of the province. The same Ralph who sat next to me at the city hall press room and regularly missed crucial votes because he was doing his own research at a bar around the corner.

My friend from Montreal who arrived in Calgary five years before I did was Harvey Cohen, his surname the most common Jewish name in any phone book. In Montreal, he would immediately be categorized according to his religion, neighbourhood and family. In Calgary, he often went unrecognized as a Jew. The name Cohen, the ancient order of Jewish priests, meant nothing to prairie people. His ethnic background wasn't nearly as important as who he was and whether you could trust him. In Alberta, society itself was on the make and willing to give anyone a chance to come along for the rodeo ride.

The white cowboy hat was the Calgary calling card, along with the top-stitched cowboy boots, embroidered shirt and jeans, even the silver six-shooter in the holster on the hip. This thousand-dollar getup was kept in the back closet most of the time but worn with pride at the big event of the year, the Calgary Stampede. Small, thin Chinese businessmen who looked like they had just arrived from Hong Kong but in fact were fourth-generation Calgarians, were as comfortable in their Stetsons as working cowhands from a roundup south of the city.

After leaving the Jewish enclave in Montreal, I had no desire to join another one in Calgary. I was anxious to shed my old, narrowly focused identity as a member of a tribe with a pre-assigned destiny. In five years in Calgary, I never went to synagogue or celebrated Jewish holidays or rituals. I simply lived as everyman, like any other newly arrived young person looking for adventure and life experience in an exciting new city.

I shared a point of reference with my workmates, a collection of young reporters on their way up or down the ladder of ambition that stretched across the country, but only reached the top rungs in Toronto. That reference point was journalism, which became a cause in itself to young, idealistic reporters covering a city on the move. If anyone was making money they shouldn't, by compromising the political process or bending the rules in their favour, we would track them down and haul them before the court of public opinion.

One lunch hour in downtown Calgary, I dropped in at the YMCA. I was looking for a place to work out, and some of my friends at the paper had recommended the Y. As I approached the front desk, men from nearby office buildings were flashing their membership cards as they rushed in. I asked the clerk about opening times and fees. He gave me a brochure describing the pool, workout machines, weight room.

"Can I look around?"

"The exercise room is right there. You get to the pool through the change room."

A few minutes later I was back.

"Can I try the place before I join?"

"Sure. I'll give you a pass."

What I was trying to figure out, but didn't know how to ask, was whether I was eligible for membership. I knew

my father and his generation were unwelcome at the
Montreal YMCA in the 1920s and '30s. In those days,
they took the "C" for Christian seriously and kept Jews
out of the club. The next day, I tried the pool and the
workout room, still wondering if they would allow me
to join. But no one asked my religion when I signed up
and paid my fees.

In Montreal, the common issues that divided us were
language, culture and religion. In Calgary, the old tightly
defined ethnic divisions of the east seemed irrelevant. No
one seemed to care who your father was, where you were
raised, what church you went to or didn't. Of course you
were expected to speak English, or "speak white" as some
French Canadians were told. But the defining questions
were, Could you be trusted? Was your word any good?
Could you make money? If religion was involved in these
issues, it was the worship of the almighty dollar.

In Montreal in the years I was growing up, we were
all French or English or Jewish or something else, all living in our tight little neighbourhoods and avoiding one
another. In Calgary, we all came from somewhere else,
maybe as far away as the Punjab or as close as Standard,
Alberta. The only territorial divisions were defined by
wealth. If you could afford a stately mansion in Mount
Royal, the old-money neighbourhood of Calgary, you
bought one, no matter how dark your skin or how thick
your accent. If anyone sneered at you, you ignored him.
Or you revved your Cadillac late at night in front of
his house.

It seemed the whole country changed in the 1970s,
but the new rules were already in place in Alberta, an
open, frontier society dripping in oil money. In 1971,

Canada became the first nation in the world to formally adopt a policy of respect of the cultures of all peoples under the clumsy label of multiculturalism. This was preceded by the Canadian Bill of Rights, and ideas like freedom and equality were finally fixed into the constitution with the Charter of Rights and Freedoms. Of course, you can pass a thousand laws about human relations, but they only have meaning if they are supported by the people who bump into each other on the street every day.

I give some credit to my own generation for creating the new Canada. We had come through the '60s and many of us had opened up to the world through travel, culture or exposure to the thousands of new immigrants who were streaming in from around the globe. Most of us came to realize that judging a person by religion, colour or ethnic background was obsolete, unproductive and just plain stupid.

In the new Canada, despite the exalted status of the founding cultures of French and English, other groups were encouraged to develop their own identities. In the last quarter of the century, the immigrants of the past gradually became the establishment of the present. You could see the change in an instant on the streets of any major Canadian city. Where once there was nothing but white faces, people of Asian and African descent had become a significant minority.

I witnessed many of these changes from Calgary, which to me seemed like the capital of Western Canada. It was all for the good. Stale, old white-bread Canada was being leavened by new influences from around the world. It's not that prejudice was unknown in Alberta, it's just that it got swept off the agenda in favour of other pursuits, like pumping oil as fast as our American cousins could burn it and building new neighbourhoods that spread over the prairie like a spring flood.

I search my memory for any anti-Jewish sentiment directed at me in five years in Calgary and come up with very little. Whatever intolerance I did encounter seemed misdirected, sometimes comically.

I was once having a meeting with an alderman named Don Hartman, something of a blusterer and a constant thorn in the mayor's side.

As we stirred our coffee cups, Hartman was muttering about the mayor, the brilliant but authoritarian Rod Sykes. Suddenly, out of nowhere, he slipped in a comment about the man's religion:

"He's a Catholic, you know."

I nodded and said nothing.

A few minutes later as we discussed the mayor's leadership style, he picked up this theme:

"Well sure, he's Catholic, that's how they are."

Then he looked at me, watery eyes through thick glasses, noticing I hadn't responded to his jibes about the mayor's religion: "You're not Catholic, are you, Sid?"

I told him I wasn't. Still in my twenties, raised in a mental ghetto that pitted Jews against the world, I barely knew the difference between Catholics and Protestants beyond belief in the Pope. According to my upbringing, what all Christians had in common was hatred of us Jews, and any minor differences among them were irrelevant. And here I was, across the table from a Protestant who was sharing his intolerance of Catholics, without realizing that I was in fact another mile across the divide, a Jew.

Or maybe he didn't see it that way. Years later, I encountered a similar sentiment. My friend Ada Cotton, a sweet, round-faced woman, recounts this story of telling her Irish Protestant mother about adopting a new religion.

"Mom, I have something to tell you. I'm going to convert."

"To what?"

"I'm going to become Jewish."

"Oh. Thank God you're not going to be a Catholic."

We Jews always feel more persecuted, more down-trodden than anyone else. So it's humorous, even a little comforting, to find that someone dislikes another group more than us.

15

HARRY AND VICTOR

D o you want the synagogue to close down?"
What a thought. I was sitting in my office at
Monday Magazine in downtown Victoria just
a block away from Congregation Emanu-El, the oldest
synagogue in Canada and the only one on Vancouver
Island.

"No, of course not," I said to the elderly man standing next to me.

"Then pay your dues. Become a member." I looked at
him, heavy eyelids behind glasses, a round wrinkled face,
balding white hair, a large belly struggling against a brass
belt buckle. He was Harry Brown, an elder of the congregation.

I had been avoiding his phone calls for days. "I don't
have my chequebook."

"I'll be back tomorrow. Bring it."

And so I was signed up as a member of Congregation
Emanu-El of Victoria, ending my separation from the
Jewish community that began during my time in Calgary.

If Harry served as the bad cop in my recruitment back into the fold, Victor Reinstein, the resident rabbi, was the good cop. Victor was in his thirties, bearded, bushy-haired, good-natured, methodical.

I had started going to cultural activities at Emanu-El, then to the occasional lecture and Saturday service. The small Jewish community of Victoria was warm and inviting, but curious. "Are you a doctor?" I was asked. "Are you a lawyer? Do you work at the university?" Why else would you be in this remote little shtetl? Jen and I had moved here in late 1979, eager for a new life-adventure on the West Coast after my career at the *Calgary Herald* hit a dead end.

On Thursday at noon, Victor led "tea and Torah," a bag-lunch discussion of the week's Torah reading. A small group of people would gather in the synagogue, which dated back to 1863, and reflect on the Biblical lessons under a blue glow of sunlight streaming through a stained glass window.

Victor taught us the meaning of the phrase *Tikkun Ha'olam*, one answer to the eternal human question, "Why are we on earth?" Here's how he explained it: When God created the world, His strength was so powerful that the vessel of creation broke into many small fragments that were scattered around the earth. *Tikkun Ha'olam*, repair of the world, is about collecting all these sacred pieces and putting the vessel back together again. Finding the pieces involves doing good deeds, the obligation of every Jewish person. The idea is, if we all work at *Tikkun*, one day the final fragment of the holy vessel will fit into place like the last piece of a jigsaw puzzle. God's creation will be complete and a great light will shine on

the world. Victor helped me see the moral side of Judaism,
which often gets lost in all the prayers and rituals and
dietary restrictions. So between Victor's carrot and Harry's stick, I was drawn back into the Jewish community.
Now, they are both gone. Victor returned to Boston so
he could raise his children in a larger Jewish community
and Harry passed on in his eighties and was laid to rest
in the historic Jewish cemetery, even older than the synagogue. When Harry's coffin was lowered into the ground,
the gravedigger bent over and his cellphone slipped out
of his shirt pocket. It couldn't be retrieved with shovels
and no one wanted to climb in, so the grave was filled in
with the cellphone on the coffin. This was an ironic twist
for a man who was always on the phone collecting for
the cause.

The Jewish songs and ceremonies appealed to my sense
of nostalgia, but Victor's teaching of the moral under-
pinning of Judaism brought me back to the community.
These ideas weren't all new to me, just reinforced and
elaborated by the rabbi and other members of the congregation. My father had taught me that all of Judaism
can be summed up in the phrase, *V'ahavtah l'reyahkhah
kamokhah*, And you shall love your neighbour as yourself. It's a direct commandment from God to Moses, in
Leviticus, chapter 19. I grew to believe this is Judaism's
greatest contribution to the world, the idea that we must
love each other and perform good works every day of
our lives.

The ethics of Judaism appealed to my sense of making the world a better place. In Victoria, I felt I could be
both everyman and Jewish at the same time. In this city,
Jews had worked with non-Jews since the mid-nineteenth

century, as merchants, builders and tradesmen. The history books talk of early Victoria as a place of cooperation among people of different ethnic backgrounds—including a black contingent that arrived in 1858—and of Jews being elected to city council and the colonial legislature. The small Jewish community didn't live apart from the rest of Victoria in the early days and it doesn't in modern times. This suited me well—I couldn't accept a form of Jewish practice that required me to return to the ghetto mentality of my early years.

The rabbi was married and had three young children. I studied with Victor during the week, and on Sunday evenings in the winter I played hockey with him and his two older children at a local arena. He was the first rabbi I ever saw wearing skates and chasing a puck around a rink.

In Victoria, I came full circle, reclaiming Judaism and adding it to the rest of my values. It usually feels like a comfortable compromise, sharing in various cultural customs including my own, similar to other people around me.

I live between two worlds, two identities, Judaism and the greater North American culture. Sometimes the distance between the two seems like a few steps. But then something will emerge to make the gap seem so wide I can barely see the other side.

We were gathered in our kitchen in Victoria on a warm summer evening. The view out the window was a burst of green foliage from my neighbour's apple tree and wild rose bushes. We had just finished a dinner of barbecued sockeye salmon with our visiting friends from back east, who I'll call Gord and Nora. We were sipping wine, recalling the delightful swim in the nearby Koksilah River that afternoon.

Gord and I were old buddies from Canadian Press days, both intensely interested in politics and public issues. The conversation drifted toward the tragic situation in the Middle East, a particularly violent phase in the conflict between Israel and the Palestinians.

"It's terrible what Israel is doing," he challenged.

"What's terrible about defending yourself against attack?"

"Come on. The Israeli army is attacking the Palestinians."

I could feel the emotional swell rising up the back of my neck. "How would you like it if someone bombed the bus you were riding on?"

"I'm not occupying and persecuting another people."

"You're not? Ask the Indians about that."

"The Indians? They're a defeated people. Anyway, we're not killing them in the streets."

Nora was starting to squirm in her seat, upset that this talk between her husband and an old friend was turning into a bitter argument.

But I kept going. "These people want to take over Israel, wipe out the Jewish state."

"But it's Israel that's wiping out the Palestinians."

"What do you expect the Jews to do—lie down and let the Arabs destroy them?"

"Who's destroying who? It's the Palestinians who are dying." Gord finished his glass and I didn't refill it.

I glared at him ten miles across the table. "Isn't it time the Jews defended themselves? Don't you know the legacy of Jewish persecution?"

"What's that got to do with it?"

"It's part of the same continuum—Jews under attack, just like they have been for centuries."

"Israel attacks other people, and you talk about the persecution of the Jews."

"But that's what it's all about. The Jews are threatened by twenty hostile Arab states. And it's just fifty years after Hitler."

"Here we go again."

"What do you mean?"

"Using the Holocaust to justify what Israel is doing in the West Bank."

"What?"

"Sure. You see it in the media all the time."

"Gord!" Nora protested, staring at him. "Stop it."

The tension rippled around the table.

I squinted in anger at my good friend of twenty-five years. "What are you talking about?"

"That's enough," she said. "You won't convince each other."

I could see Nora was right. This discussion was heading down a dark hole where an old friendship could disappear. A pitched argument wasn't appropriate after-dinner discussion for two friends on a summer evening with their spouses suffering on the sidelines. We went back to talk of the swim in the river and our plans for the next day. I suppressed my anger, but I looked at my friend differently, with frustration and suspicion.

That night as I lay down to sleep I was still seething. The Holocaust is sacred. A non-Jew can't throw it in the face of a Jew to make a political point. How could he? I festered, my eyes open in the near-darkness. Gord was one of my best friends, but here we were, on opposite sides of an argument that touched on the most sensitive of Jewish nerve endings—the existence of the state of Israel and the legacy of the Holocaust. Yes, it was me who brought the two issues together, but he accused me of cynically using Hitler's genocide to advance the cause of Israel. How much meaning could I read into what he said? Was I part of some conspiracy because this argument was "in the media all the time"? We were old friends; we agreed on almost every issue. Why were we so far apart on the Middle East? And why was he so dismissive of my concern over the Arab threat to the existence of the state of Israel?

This gap in perception of the Middle East struggle is a sharp point of distinction between Jews and non-Jews. Other friends of mine also take the Palestinian side and ignore the death of Israelis, the threat to Israel. Can't they see? The Palestinians are the proxy fighters in a war against Israel waged by powerful Arab and Muslim states. The hostility of these people is virulent enough to bring about another Holocaust, this time against the state of Israel. The hatred and the will are there, it's just a matter of the method and the ability. And many people, including some of my close friends, sit on the sidelines and blame the Jews.

And of course, for me the threat to Israel was a very personal matter. It was where my parents lived, as well as other relatives. My distant cousin Sophia and her family had recently left the Russian homeland, still oppressive and anti-Semitic sixty years after my grandparents fled. The fact that Jews from all over the world, persecuted and evicted from other countries, should finally re-establish their own homeland and are threatened there as well, is infuriating to Jews everywhere.

People who aren't Jewish ignore the depth of the

hatred in the region, the imminent threat that Jews see from the Arab states. And they're tired of us bringing up the spectre of the Holocaust, like an old soldier unbuttoning his shirt to show the scars of his terrible war wound. Perhaps they're right, perhaps we tell too many stories of people herded into gas chambers, about the next pogrom around the corner the Jews are always expecting. Maybe we do repeat the story excessively, but six million people was excessive. Give us a few hundred years to get over it.

Call me hyper-sensitive, but a non-Jew, especially a Christian, can't turn the Holocaust finger back at us. Not if he understands the responsibility of the church in the legacy of hatred and murder that led to the Nazi genocide. It was the priests and bishops who preached hatred against the Jews for centuries, who carried the torches leading the mobs to the Jewish quarter to purge the non-believers who rejected the gift of Christian conversion.

I have noticed this tendency among human beings all my life: an acute awareness of our own persecution and blindness to the suffering of others. We just can't summon the same sense of urgency to speak out or take action when it's another people who are being persecuted. It is a factor of my own identity that I know and feel the pain of the Jewish people. Of course, the persecutors of the Jews have given me much to know and feel. But why can't other people identify with this legacy of oppression? Perhaps for the same reason that I can't react to the suffering of others with the same sense of outrage and compassion.

Ignoring or denying the persecution of other people is a basic human flaw. You can find the pressure point of

Jewish conscience by citing the Palestinians as an example. Some Jews will deny Palestinian suffering under Israeli occupation or redirect blame and responsibility. But other Jews, including some Israelis, work every day to advance the Palestinian cause.

Empathy is a watchword of the modern, evolved human being. Many people can detect its absence in anyone but themselves. In an age of instant global connection, we are often called upon to face the tragedies of others, perhaps so often that we tend to ignore them.

If you're Jewish you care deeply about the Holocaust. If you're not, you may try to understand, or maybe, you don't know, don't want to know, or perhaps, don't believe it. What's six million Jews, one in every three, murdered by Hitler in the Second World War? To us, it's the great tragedy of the millennium; to them, just another ugly chapter of the bloody legacy of the last century.

To many people, the Holocaust is the epitome of man's inhumanity to man. But what of the Turkish slaughter of the Armenians a half-century before? Or the more recent massacres in Yugoslavia, in Rwanda, Cambodia, Darfur? And closer to home, in historical times, aboriginal people of the Americas? The list could go on. The traditional Jewish response is there is no hierarchy of mass murder, all are horrific. But we focus on ours and insist it is uniquely terrible.

Is it the same with other national tragedies? Do only those who belong to the group who were persecuted really care? Surely the Holocaust and other such tragedies must be seen as crimes against humanity that affect every living human being on earth.

16

THE LAND OF GOD'S PROMISE

The man sitting next to me on the bus was lean and black, his skin folded into the wrinkles on his face. I guessed he was sixty-five, his hair barely touched with grey but his face weathered. The bus was shaking up the highway from Tel Aviv to Haifa, spewing diesel fumes, lurching to a stop for passengers every few miles. My wife Jen and I were travelling on this busy highway to see my cousin Sophia in the midst of a visit with my parents.

The bus was crowded and there were no empty seats together when we got on, so I sat next to the black man and Jen took a seat a few rows behind us. The man stared straight ahead as I peeked at him and finally caught his attention.

"Are you going to Haifa?" I asked in Hebrew.

"No, just before Haifa."

"Are you visiting family?"

"My son."

A minute later, he returned the question. "And you?"

"North of Haifa, to visit a cousin."

"Where are you from?"

"Canada."

We exchanged short phrases and sentences. Hebrew was a second language for both of us and neither spoke it well.

He was a recent immigrant, part of a rescue airlift of Ethiopian Jews separated from the larger community of Judaism for a thousand years or more. He was one of my people, but we could hardly be more different: a dark-skinned African from a rural area of one of the poorest countries in the world and a white North American from one of the most comfortable cities in the First World.

Is this man really Us, I wondered. His culture is known as Falasha, an ancient, mysterious offshoot of Judaism. Their origins are uncertain, but they claim to be descendants of King Solomon and the Queen of Sheba. Their very identity and bona fides as Jews were in doubt and carefully studied by Israeli rabbis before they were finally recognized as legitimate Jewish immigrants.

The bus left a suburban area north of Tel Aviv and the driver accelerated up a straightaway. To the left, the gentle surf of the blue Mediterranean came into view, an invitation to a day on the beach. We pulled to a stop and three young soldiers got on, carrying machine guns, a typical sight in Israel. I prayed silently that the bus would not be attacked by a suicide bomber on this day.

I glanced at the man beside me again. He was still looking straight ahead, not at the ocean view. We had everything and nothing in common. To start, we were both human beings and adult males in the latter half of life. To end, we were both Jews. But it would take an interpreter and a great effort to begin to understand each others' lives. We were destined to never go beyond this brief and simple conversation.

"How many children do you have?" I asked.

"Four." Then a moment later, "How many do you have?"

"Two." I really had none, but I offered a little white lie to a black man I would never see again. I imagined he would have pitied me had I told the truth. The bare thread between us would have broken, the gap between us widened even further. He would have considered me an even more exotic creature than I was.

Over the ages, many Jews yearned to travel to Israel but never got the chance. I've been there so many times I've lost track. More than twenty is my best guess.

The visits to Israel were meant to compensate for my mother's loneliness. For thirty years, we travelled there every second year and my parents came to Canada the other year. Later, as Dad became ill, they stopped travelling and we went every year, even twice a year.

I came to see Israel, and especially Kfar Menachem, as my second home, a place of pride and belonging. The kibbutz was a working farm of chickens, cattle and field crops and a garden of exotic plants and trees—bougainvillea, jacaranda, plumeria, and a strange African tree with lovely pink flowers and needle-sharp spikes on the trunk. And my parents' home was a sanctuary of the heart, where my mother would be waiting with her warm smile and a plate of poppy-seed cookies, a favourite since childhood.

Other people just drive across town to see their parents. I had to travel around the world, assuring my friends I wouldn't be murdered in a terrorist attack, feeling less than certain myself. I walked a gauntlet of bloodthirsty people who would kill me because I was travelling to the Zionist entity. I wished I could tell them, "Please, I'm only visiting my old mother."

In the blackness of night, the jackals howled. I lay in bed, straining to hear the high-pitched yelps in the distance. Jen slept beside me. The calling grew louder—keening, maniacal, with an eerie, almost human quality. I imagined the jackals roaming the hills bragging of their latest kill. Their calls are a reminder of the untamed forces beyond the fenced perimeter of the kibbutz—the snake, the thistle, the stony plain, the Bedouin on his donkey.

I was jet-lagged, awake in the middle of the night after the twenty-four-hour flight to Israel. I was coughing in fits, a bug picked up on the plane. I got up, switched on the light in the bathroom and leaned over the faucet to wash down a sleeping pill. I returned to bed and waited for the pill to take effect. I suppressed a cough, but it welled up from my chest to my throat. The jackals in the hills were laughing at me, a foreigner wide awake in their land at their time of night. Their calls grew distant and I drifted off.

The next morning after breakfast I arrived at the kibbutz medical clinic seeking treatment for my hacking cough. At 9 a.m. in early spring the sun was already searing the concrete porch as I opened the glass door.

"Can I see the doctor?" I asked the severe-looking nurse with wiry black hair tied back in a bun.

"Yes."

"When?"

"Soon." She closed the door behind her.

I sat in the waiting room, well named. "Soon" passed and passed again. Patients filed in and out, called by name by the nurse's assistant.

Israeli public services are bound by bureaucracy, and in this small medical office, the codes of access and priority were regulated with measured discretion by the nurse in charge.

The room was square and furnished with chairs and a sofa, chilled by a humming air conditioner and decorated with posters offering advice to pregnant women. When the inner door opened, I timed a coughing fit for the nurse. She ignored me. A half-hour later, I noticed a kibbutz member checking a typewritten list of names and appointment times tacked to the door. My name wasn't on the list.

A young man and two young women arrived. One of the women was holding a baby boy, perhaps six months old. The man carried himself with confidence and was short, broad, well-built, with striking emerald green eyes. I guessed he was the father, the woman holding the child the mother. Was the other woman her sister or his? The nurse's assistant approached them and they exchanged a few words. Another woman, a kibbutz member waiting her turn, gurgled at the black-haired baby. The young man and two women chatted with each other. But they weren't speaking Hebrew. I didn't understand a word. Then I realized they were Arabs from the neighbouring village, attending the closest medical clinic to their home.

In a few moments, they were ushered in. It seemed

the game of favouritism, or *protectzia* as it is known in Israel, was being played to their benefit. So much for preferential treatment for Jews in Israel. All three adults and the child disappeared into the doctor's office. This is family medicine, I thought. The father, mother and sister were all involved in the child's care. Fifteen minutes later, the door opened and they left, smiling and chatting. Finally, the doctor saw me, the last and least of the patients.

Quite simply, the Arab family got to see the doctor before me because they knew the protocol and I didn't. Whether that meant they called ahead to make an appointment or they were given priority as a special courtesy to the neighbours, I wasn't sure. I was bemused by this incident, intrigued by the politics of the waiting room. What struck me was how unimaginable this scene would appear to those who think Jews and Arabs in the Middle East spend all their time at each others' throats. In Israel, a Jewish doctor examining an Arab baby is actually a more typical interaction, but largely unknown in the rest of the world.

It was a hot September evening in the land of God's promise, a year after my visit to the medical clinic. The setting sun cast a soft glow on rows of grain on either side of the dusty road. I was travelling in a blue pickup over a back road behind Kfar Menachem with Yehuda Karon. He was in charge of the kibbutz field crops, a handsome, compact man of fifty-five with bright blue eyes and a day's growth of stubble.

The road dipped and curved, then crossed a rail line as we approached a farming settlement—a few tall houses, animal enclosures, a large shed for tractors and harvest-ers. This was the compound of the family of Younis al-Azzi, the closest neighbours to the kibbutz, and we were paying a visit. Yehuda had inherited the role of main contact with the al-Azzi family from his father David who had died a few years earlier. This was my first trip to the Arab neighbours in twenty years of visits to Kfar Menachem, my first chance to meet these people. The Jews of the kibbutz and the Arabs in this village have lived in peace here for sixty years, in times of celebration and other times of grave danger.

The buildings were large, two and three storeys built on pilings with an empty space where the ground floor would have been, as if they were expecting a flood. A few goats chewed on rough, sage-coloured bushes. As we climbed out of the truck, a group of small boys eyed us warily and then resumed playing in the yard.

Three men approached Yehuda with smiles, hugs and handshakes. He introduced me in Hebrew, the language they share. We sat at a white plastic patio table and one of the men brought a metal pot of sweet, flowery tea, which he poured into small glasses. Cattle grazed in an adjacent field in the fading light. The sun dropped to the horizon, a mesmerizing colour of deep red and gold. The area around the homes was rich green lawn, a sprinkler spraying a wide swath in a slow, circular motion. A blue peacock pecked at the grass.

"*Ma neeshma?*" asked the youngest of the three, a short, strongly built man. "How's it going?"

The conversation was fast, the Hebrew staccato bouncing back and forth across the table. I caught much of it, but lost some nuance and detail. Yehuda folded his arms and the three sons of Younis al-Azzi interlaced their fingers. I studied the brothers, their similarities and differences. They seemed relaxed, proud, self-assured. The youngest might be mid-thirties, the oldest, fifty. They spoke Hebrew with comfort and ease, far better than me, inflecting the words with Arabic accents. The oldest brother was tall and thin, the middle brother dark and talkative and quick with a smile, the youngest shorter with flashing green eyes—then I recognized him as the man with the baby at the clinic the year before.

The older brother, the reserved patriarch, is called Rommel, to me an unusual Arabic name. Later, Yehuda explained he was named after the legendary German general who fought the Allies in North Africa in the Second World War. Different people, different war heroes. His father, Younis, who died thirty years earlier, was nicknamed Abu Rommel, father of Rommel, a title to honour his oldest son. This is an Arabic custom, a tight knot in the family ties. Despite his death long ago, this little settlement was still known on the kibbutz as "the house of Younis."

At first, the men talked about farming, tending their crops.

"When will you harvest?" asked Yehuda.

"Soon. The crop is ready," Rommel said.

I slipped in a question to the three men across the table. "How do you get along with the people on the kibbutz? Are you friends?"

The middle one smiled. "*Lo chaverim, achim.* Not friends, brothers. We have lived side by side for many years."

And what of the intifada, the war that was raging between the Israelis and the Palestinians in the Occupied Territories?

"*Balagan!*" This is a particularly Israeli idiom that means turmoil, confusion, brought on by stupidity. But his one-word description avoided blaming either side.

"What's the solution? Should there be a separate state for the Palestinians?"

"No, everyone should live together," he said and stopped. In the Middle East, every word about Arab-Israeli relations is checked like a suspicious package for hidden meaning and nuance. Did he mean peace and cooperation in a binational state or an Arab-dominated Palestine to replace Jewish Israel? The brow of the golden sun rested on the horizon, sinking slowly. I finished my tea and the middle brother refilled my glass.

Then the conversation became more animated as the three brothers told Yehuda of an incident in their village a few days before. A Palestinian infiltrator from the West Bank, perhaps looking for a day's work in Israel, was arrested by the Israeli border police, the Mishmar Ha'gvul. As the police gave chase, lights flashing red, the man fled on foot onto the al-Azzi family compound. Perhaps he recognized an Arab enclave. The police drove their Jeeps onto the soft green lawn to apprehend the fleeing man and roughed him up before hauling him away.

During the height of the intifada, there were strict limitations on border crossing from the West Bank as the Israeli military tried to shut down terrorist attacks. But hundreds of West Bank Palestinians, their own economy in shambles, tried to sneak into Israel to find work, usually menial day labour.

This was a pointed lesson in the complexity of the struggle in the Middle East. The al-Azzi farm is located in Israel, and the family members are peaceful, productive members of Israeli society. But they are ethnically

identical to Palestinian Arabs living twenty miles away
in the West Bank, who were at war with Israel. The
al-Azzis even have relatives in the West Bank—the
connections are as close as cousins of a Canadian family
living in two adjacent provinces. The Israeli army con-
quered the West Bank from Jordan in 1967, and has held
it ever since. The Palestinians who live there are under
military rule, while the al-Azzis and more than a million
other Arabs in Israel itself live in relative freedom, peace
and prosperity.

On this evening under the setting sun, this entire saga
was reduced to a single complaint: the al-Azzi brothers
were upset that the Israeli police Jeeps invaded their property and that the infiltrator was manhandled in view of
their wives and children.

"This shouldn't happen," the middle brother said to
Yehuda. "This is an affront."

"Yes, you're right, *meah achuz*, a hundred per cent,"
Yehuda replied. He told them to go to the border police
station in the nearby town of Kiryat Malachi and complain to the commanding officer. The three brothers
looked doubtful.

No one seemed concerned about the fate of the arrested man. The offence seemed to have been committed
against the family, which was forced to witness the arrest
on their lawn, rather than the man who was hauled off
to jail. This sentiment seemed to transcend ethnic blood-
lines, the fact that the arrested infiltrator and the al-Azzis
are all Palestinian Arabs.

I am the outsider here, with limited grasp of the language and the conflict. But it occurs to me, Yehuda and
the al-Azzi brothers share something that sets them apart

from Arab refugees in the West Bank or poor Jewish immigrants in Israeli cities: they are landed, established,
successful. They live in comfortable homes surrounded
by gardens and tend crops on large rolling farms that
stretch as far as the eye can see. Arabs and Jews, they are
the winners in the battle for supremacy in the Middle
East. Because winning or losing depends on whether your
children go to bed hungry, not which political master sits
in the capital. No wonder they are good neighbours.

But of course there are winners and losers in every
society. The ideal of a socialist utopia, of nothing but
winners, is a distant memory around the world—even
on the kibbutz, where the allure of personal gain is quickly
replacing collectivist ideals. The goal now is much more
narrowly defined than creating the ideal, egalitarian society envisaged by the founders of the kibbutz—it's that
Israelis and Palestinians can just get along, live in peace
side by side. These men are an example of that, a lesson
for millions of Arabs and Jews who can't see beyond their
fear and hatred.

The sun sank below the horizon and darkness began
to settle over the land. We must get back to the kibbutz,
Yehuda told his friends. No hurry, said one of the brothers, stay for a coffee. "*Kos café.*" It sounded enticing
in Hebrew with an Arabic inflection. The tea arrived
automatically, but the coffee required an invitation,
an announcement. I imagined spices and scents, sweet
pastries and plush cushions inside the house. I felt the
warmth of hospitality, of welcome to the stranger,
wrapped in a tradition and culture I barely understand.

"*Kos café,*" the middle brother offered again with a
smile and a gesture.

"*Ohd pa'am,*" said Yehuda. "Another time."

As we stood to leave, we met another man carrying a curly-haired baby in his sleeper. Yehuda coddled the baby and I took a picture. We saw women at a distance, but they remained there. We walked to our truck and another man arrived and pumped Yehuda's hand and clapped his shoulder. There was laughter and warmth in a round of handshakes as we extended our goodbyes into the darkness. The warmth was in the air as well, after 7 p.m. in late September, still sultry, short-sleeve weather. As we drove slowly back over the farm road, rising from a dip in the land to cross the rail line, I chatted with Yehuda and then my mind drifted back to the brothers al-Azzi. Then to the verse from Psalms, set to music as an Israeli folk song,

"*Hine ma tov u ma nayim, shevet achim gam yachad,*
How good and how pleasant, brothers all living together."

The day after our trip to the village, I met Yehuda over cold fruit juice in his home, overlooking the fields of grain and fruit trees he cultivates. He told the story of sixty years of neighbourly relations between the kibbutz and the al-Azzi family. He called it "a small peace."

In the 1940s before the creation of the state of Israel, Kfar Menachem survived as a small Jewish outpost surrounded by mostly hostile Arabs, partly due to the support and protection of the al-Azzi family. Younis, the patriarch, saw the arrival of hard-working Jewish settlers and the modern farming methods they brought as a positive force in the desolate lands of south-central Palestine. He wasn't alone among Arabs and Jews who envisioned a new independent country of cooperation and goodwill among all its peoples. Straining under the yoke of the British, who ruled the area for thirty years, Arab and Jewish idealists dreamed of an independent binational state, where they would live and work hand in hand.

But there was also strife and ill will on both sides, and history turned in another direction when the UN voted in 1947 to divide Palestine into two countries, one Arab, one Jewish. The front-line Arab nations rejected this plan and attacked the emerging Jewish state in what became the Israeli War of Independence. Many Arabs living in Israel fled to neighbouring Arab countries, fearful of being caught in the crossfire.

Yehuda fills in the details of the fate of the al-Azzi family during that time. Younis spent two nights sheltered on Kfar Menachem, then slipped away to refuge among his own people. He and his family crossed into Jordan, where they lived for several years in Hebron and Bethlehem on the West Bank. The kibbutz members took care of the al-Azzi farm and kept it intact in their absence. In the early 1950s, Yehuda's father David Karon, who spoke fluent Arabic, helped the al-Azzis return to their lands bordering the kibbutz.

Over the years, the al-Azzi family compound grew to a small village. Younis had several wives who bore eight sons and five daughters and they all had their own families. Younis and his friend David Karon are long gone. But the children of these two men maintain the trust they established during turbulent times. Just a few miles away, the *balagan* raged, but here a small peace endured.

For years, as I visited my parents on Kfar Menachem, the Arab enclave a few miles away remained a mirage of

shimmering structures on the horizon. The kibbutz has
been here, on a rolling plain below the Judean Hills, since
1939. Throughout the years, there has never been a shot
fired across these fields, never a drop of blood shed in
anger, although war is both near and recent among friends
and relatives on both sides. These are Arabs and Jews
living in a complicated harmony, as they do in much of
Israel, where Arabs form twenty per cent of the population and Arabic is an official language.

My mother told me of travelling to the al-Azzi compound with the kibbutz doctor when she was a younger
woman. The doctor inoculated several newborn babies.
My mother, who had worked in the nursery on the kibbutz and loves babies, held them in her arms and comforted them when they cried at the prick of the needle.

Another time, she went with my father to a wedding
in the Arab village. Belly dancers swayed to the pounding drumbeat, tent cloth billowed in the breeze, people
feasted at tables laden with food and drink. The bride
was of the al-Azzi family, perhaps the daughter of Younis.
The groom was from the West Bank, just twenty miles
away—or was it a million miles? The family invited hundreds of people from the area, plus friends and relatives
from distant places. The al-Azzi family has connections
across the Middle East, in Europe, even Canada. The
hosts were careful to follow the dietary laws of their
guests: wine for the Jews, but not for the Muslims; food
of the Arab tradition for family and friends; kosher
Israeli-style food for the Jews. The guests from the
kibbutz went home late, some tipsy. There was no anger,
no hatred. It's how you'd expect neighbours to behave,
even better. Few families anywhere would invite

several hundred people from the neighbourhood to their daughter's wedding.

On my last visit to Kfar Menachem, the al-Azzis had invited the kibbutz old-timers, the pioneers who were now in their eighties and nineties, to their village to reminisce about years gone by. Yehuda arranged the visit. "Many years pass and you forget the things you've taken for granted. They just wanted to see some of these people again, to talk about old times."

My good friend Dina, a German Jew who escaped Hitler's clutches and arrived on the kibbutz in 1939 a few months before the war, was one of the group of twenty who drank coffee and chatted with the al-Azzi family.

"You can trust them," she told me. "If I was in trouble, I would go to them." In the Middle East, where trouble is a constant threat, trust between Arab and Jewish neighbours is a precious commodity.

For many years, I have thought, the world should see Kfar Menachem and its neighbouring Arab village. The world should see Arab police officers, businesspeople, lawyers and doctors, Arab members of the Israeli Knesset or parliament. It's not a perfect society, there is hostility and prejudice. But if there is one country in the Middle East where Jews and Arabs live side by side in peace, it is Israel.

17

HALLOWED MAY HE BE

On the kibbutz, my father was fulfilling his dream of living the communal life in the land of his forefathers. But that wasn't enough—he wanted to fulfill other people's dreams as well. He was full of ideas and advice, which he tried to put across in his limited Hebrew. The kibbutz needed new leadership, new strategies, special incentives to encourage members. Built on strict socialist principles, the kibbutz gave each member identical benefits—housing, food and a small stipend—regardless of which job they did. The general manager got the same pay as the man or woman who mopped the dining-room floors. Dad wanted to introduce incentives and bonuses, a revolutionary step for the kibbutz.

The ideas buzzed in his mind. Kfar Menachem, the entire kibbutz movement, needed saving and there he was with the answers. Young people were leaving for the excitement and opportunities of the cities—Tel Aviv, Haifa,

Stockholm, New York. The sense of sacrifice to create a new society was dying. Kibbutz members became absorbed in material goods—a television, a car, a bigger home—rather than the interests of the community.

Dad's ideas about restoring kibbutz spirit, keeping young people down on the farm, were ignored. Who was he, a newcomer who never sweated and sacrificed through the tough years, to tell the old-timers how to reform their society? Even in English, his personality was more suited to giving orders than drawing consensus. In Hebrew, he could barely get his ideas across.

Frustrated, he drew into himself and his ever loyal wife. Age started to diminish him, his eyesight began to fail. He lost his strength and mobility to a stroke, then another stroke. He sat for hours in his black easy chair, writing letters and reading, then listening to books on tape as his eyes weakened.

He had given up so much for the kibbutz dream—his home and family, thirty years of his life—but now it was fading. The old ideal of labour as its own value, of Jews cultivating the land and building the country, had become as outdated as the mule-drawn plow. Foreign guest-workers from Thailand, the Philippines, Romania worked the fields and built the houses, took care of the children and the old folks, while the members gradually became managers, overseers, pencil-pushers. There was talk of granting private ownership to individual homes or even dividing up the kibbutz among the members. Some of the old *chalutzim*, the pioneers from the shtetls, grew bitter. *"Zeh lo kibbutz,"* said Berchik, a ninety-year-old with flashing blue eyes. "This is not kibbutz." The idea of a new society built on equality and cooperation, a shining example to the world, was dying in the very soil where it took root only fifty years before.

Abe became a silent man. It was hard to tell whether it was due to his illness or his disappointment. "When I have something to say, I say it," he told me. The man who had always taken centre stage now watched, his eyes scanning the faces of those around him talking. During one of my visits, a speaker was invited to discuss new ways to reform and run the kibbutz. Dad struggled to the meeting with his cane. The speaker rattled on in Hebrew about pay incentives and other ideas Abe had put forward years before. Silently, he took to his feet and hobbled out of the room while the man was still speaking.

★

The mourners gathered on a rocky plateau facing a field of sunflowers. It was a warm day in March 2000, the sunlight casting a honey glow on the Judean Hills in the distance. A few men stepped forward to carry the coffin to the graveside. "He was a man who believed in dreams," I read from my notes. "And he lived his dream of coming to Israel, to the kibbutz, to fulfill his life and help build a new society."

Abe had grown weak from old age and illness, but his death at 86 was a shock nonetheless. Jen and I had arrived for a visit a few days before and it seemed like he chose this time so we would be there with Sarah.

The nurse had called me to the medical clinic with the news that he had passed away during the night. It was left to me to tell Sarah. His death hit my mother like a crushing blow, the strong, decisive man she had depended on all her adult life suddenly gone, another deep level of separation from her family. She would be left alone on the kibbutz, her children and grandchildren halfway across the world.

I had to suppress my own grieving, to mask my sorrow and comfort my mother. With my father gone, it was my role to be strong and supportive, and with no rabbi on the kibbutz, to give the eulogy at his funeral.

I spoke in English and our family friend Yisrael translated to Hebrew. "He loved nature, he loved to see the birds in the trees. Just the day before he died, he was watching the migrating cranes in the branches above his room." On cue, a flock of these white birds drifted past high in the sky above the burial ground.

The men lowered the coffin into the grave and I stepped forward to recite the Kaddish, the blessing for the dead. I solemnly spoke the ancient Aramaic words in praise of God, "*Yisgadal viyis-kadash shmei raba*, Hallowed and enhanced may He be." I suddenly realized that none of the fifty people assembled was reciting the response to the prayer. In the midst of the heartland of Israel, these people, these Jews, were so divorced from traditional practice that even the simple religious ritual of laying a man to rest was unknown to them.

My father gave up his family, his way of life, but he also gave up the practice of Judaism when he moved to the land of the Jews. In Canada, he ate kosher food, prayed in the synagogue every week and observed the rituals. In Israel, he joined a secular community where even Yom Kippur, the supreme Jewish holiday, was just another workday. Strict socialist ideology would tolerate no rivals to its claim on the mind and spirit of kibbutzniks.

These people practise no religious rituals, yet they represent the backbone of Jewish culture and identity in the world today and the best hope for the survival of the people. They are Jews by birthright and commitment, by the blood in their veins and the ground that they walk on, not by observance or belief. It seems Jewish identity is so strong and deep-rooted that it can survive without its most basic tenets, without Torah, without God. Or can it?

I remember asking Abe how he could abandon the religious practice that was so important to him in Canada. "Living in Israel is my Judaism," was how he explained it. Once he moved to Israel, he no longer needed to pray or practise the rituals. He crossed the Jordan River and washed away his sins.

The men shovelled hard dry earth over the grave. We turned away and I led my mother back to the waiting car.

The next day I returned to the cemetery alone. I passed the monument to the relatives of kibbutz members who perished in the Holocaust, rows of black name plaques posted on a stone wall. It was quiet now, except for birds chirping in the trees, the sound of a tractor rumbling in the distance. I walked to the fresh grave near the edge of the cemetery.

"Dad." I repeated it over and over. "Dad. Dad. Dad." I don't know what I expected. Perhaps I would get the answers in death that I never got in life. Who was this big man? What did he want? Did he really love the woman he uprooted from her home, the children he left behind? How could a man so devoted to his family put it all aside?

We are all a tangle of contradictions, of love and loyalty mixed with doubt and indifference and hostility, of motivations and reasons we can hardly understand, let alone explain to others. And then it's all over quickly and left to those who remain to figure it out.

Over the weeks that followed, some ideas came to me. Abe had to be strong and persistent to face his trials early in life. He knocked on doors that never opened, stood up to hatred and prejudice, even to Hitler when he boycotted the Olympic Games. Perhaps this shell of strength numbed him to feeling, in himself and for others. For me, it meant he couldn't give the love I wanted or receive the love I tried to give. And of course I fear he passed on this shell to me. Men carry a lot of weight on their shoulders. They are expected to be strong, competitive and steadfast most of the time, tender and loving and vulnerable at other times. Few can measure up on both ends of the emotional scale.

By moving to Israel, Abe left his world behind and started over. Some people chart their own course early in life, others never do. Abe did it at fifty-six. He finally got to live his life his way—even if he had to break up his family to do it. He sacrificed the small tribe to join the greater tribe in a new land far away.

18

TOWER OF BABEL

The flight back home from Tel Aviv is crowded, tedious, the Air Canada crew dealing with different languages and cultural gaps, kosher and non-kosher and vegetarian meals. A third of the passengers are black-hatted Orthodox men and their families. The crew has to sidestep the religious men assembled in the aisles at the back of the plane to *daven Shacharit*, recite the morning prayer. I wonder about the time zones we're speeding through at five hundred miles per hour and whether the prayer should be repeated several times in the extended sunrise.

Later, tired of sitting, I walk back to the service counter in the rear of the plane and strike up a conversation with a tall, stout man in his mid-thirties with a light brown beard, a *kipa* or skullcap and *peyes*, side curls.

He lives in Jerusalem and is going to New York. He asks me where I'm going.

"Victoria."

He shakes his head and shrugs.

"It's on the west coast of Canada. Near Vancouver."

He shakes his head again.

"Near Seattle." A glimmer of recognition.

He takes a drink of water, then looks back at me.

"It's a small place, where you're from?"

"Yes."

"You have a Jewish community there?"

"Yes, a small one. We pray in the oldest shul in Canada, nearly a hundred and forty years old." He's not impressed. That's old where I come from, but not where he comes from.

"Do you have a lot of intermarriage?"

"Some."

"It's a terrible thing," he says, frowning. "We are losing our nation."

I don't tell him my own wife of twenty years is sitting a few rows up from us, guardian of our tickets, passports and inflatable pillows, because she would never lose them but I would. This woman who, along with me, is the light of my mother's life. Who rolls matzo balls between her hands and sets out parsley and gefilte fish on paper plates for our community Passover Seder in Victoria. Who sings my grandfather's tunes to the Seder songs along with me: *chad gadya, chad gadya.* She never converted to Judaism, but she understands many of the intricacies of the culture, Yiddish, Hebrew, the deep bond with Israel. I return to my seat where she is reading. We smile and share a kiss. When the plane lands a few hours later, we ease ahead in the crush and I barely catch the man's eye as we disembark. I can't tell if he sees me with my wife and recognizes me as one of the terrible who are destroying our nation.

To this man, I am barely one of Us, a lost Jew who may never be redeemed. And I feel equally distant from him. He is one of my people, but he seems narrow-minded and arrogant, a one-way believer. As an Orthodox Jew, he lives his entire life according to Jewish law, nearly every waking moment dedicated to ritual and observance. In some ways I envy his assurance, firmly convinced of his place in his community and the world. I am caught between two worlds, pulled between my Jewish and everyman identities. And I grapple with the very idea of Us and Them and wonder who fits into which category.

So who is this Us? And who are these Them? To many people, it's simple. Us is my tribe, my nation, my religion, my people. Everyone else is Them, and it's often "to hell with them." When I was a child, I saw the world in these simple terms, raised in a ghetto of place and mind. But I grew out of childhood and saw more complex patterns in the world—and became confused.

Sometimes I feel there is no us, only me. We are all alone in the world, millions of people isolated in the huge swell of humanity, staring up for answers at the stars in the black sky. We are sometimes surprised to discover that other people feel like outsiders, strangers, just like we do.

When I let my personal history fade to background noise, I realize we are all one species, as similar to each other as a teeming school of fish in the ocean. In terms of our journey through time on this planet, we only recently emerged from Africa, the original home of our species. We are all descendants of African primates, some with skin tones adapted to newly discovered habitats. As we migrated around the world, we learned a thousand different languages, the punishment of the Tower of Babel. After a hundred thousand years of wandering and diverging, we look and sound terribly strange to one another. The truth is, we are all very similar, though all we see are differences.

Imagine a New Guinea tribesman, never out of his small corner of the world deep in the jungle. Suddenly he is transported to—a fitness centre in New York. All those men and women in skimpy clothes attached to gleaming machines, turning and twisting to strange music. Would he stare in wonder or flee in terror?

The anthropologists argue whether mankind arrived in the Americas twelve thousand or twenty thousand years ago, all just small degrees on the scale of human history. What do we all have in common? Everything. If you saw a flock of crows flying by, they'd all look the same to you, just like us. We are all basically identical, we laugh and cry and sing and dance to music. We all hate having our skin cut, it makes us bleed. We can all express the most tender love or vicious hatred for our fellow humans. We have it in our power to create paradise on earth, instead of wishing for it in heaven. But we don't. We separate, we differentiate, we declare ourselves superior to others. We choose Us over Them in life, in death, in war and peace, wealth and starvation.

When I hitchhiked through Europe as a young man, the people in the northern part of a country would sometimes warn me about the people in the south. Be careful. Don't trust them. They'll steal from you. Some even advised me to cross the border and travel through a neighbouring country to avoid the southern part of their own country. What was in the south, I wondered. What dangers and mysteries awaited me? Trolls? Hijackers?

Marauding savages with blood dripping from their lips? To me, a southern Italian looked and sounded the same as a northern Italian. To them, there was a world of difference. To me, Italy is Italy. To them, it's Milan, Rome, Naples—they only became one country in the mid-nineteenth century. And don't even mention Sicily or Sardinia.

Once I asked one of these people if he had ever been to the south, a hundred miles from where we stood. Of course not, he said. He wouldn't think of going there. The south was a state of mind, I decided, representing their own baser emotions and tendencies, perhaps the southern part of their bodies. That's what racism often is, a reflection of our anxiety over the devil within us.

So how do we learn our attitudes toward people different from ourselves? It usually starts in childhood, when ideas are passed around among kids and sometimes get filtered through their parents.

Richard Inglis is an anthropologist who visits historic Friendly Cove off the west coast of Vancouver Island with his family every summer. I got to know him through my work as a reporter and my travels to west coast villages. Over the years, Richard has formed warm relations with the Mowachaht, descendants of the people encountered by famed British explorer James Cook, the first European to land on British Columbia's shores. Some of the Mowachaht women have become surrogate aunts to Richard's daughter. The young girl has danced with the native people, shared meals with them, played with children her age.

One day back in the city, when the girl was about six, she came home and told her father the kids in the schoolyard had been talking about Indians. "What's an

Indian?" she asked Richard. He tried to explain the difference between Indians and white people. She didn't understand. He used an example: the people we visit in Friendly Cove, they're Indians. "No, they're *not!*" his daughter replied. The little girl had already picked up negative impressions of Indians from her classmates. The wonderful people she knew in Friendly Cove didn't fit the description she heard in the schoolyard. They couldn't possibly be Indians.

I have encountered this way of thinking often in life, not among little girls, but among adults who should know better. The people we dislike are Them, an anonymous group living there, somewhere. But the individual people we know, our friends and acquaintances, they're okay. They, as a group, are not to be trusted, but that woman on the street whose kids play with our kids, nothing wrong with her. She may be one of Them, but we know her, she's all right. It's as if contact with us has somehow removed the stain. Or maybe, one day, we suddenly discover that a person we've known for years is one of Them. Catholics. Jews. Gays. We never knew. How could it be? He seemed okay to us.

It's like the hard-core racists in the southern U.S. in the 1950s. There was nothing wrong with the black folks they knew. They wanted everyone to get along. They just wanted the races living apart, the whites in the good neighbourhoods, the blacks in the slums. Black folks were fine, as long as they behaved like they always did and knew their place.

I once knew a man who was an anti-Semite, or talked like one. I know that sounds ambiguous, but I was confused. We were thrown together in work and he expressed some odious ideas about Jews, black people, and other groups different from himself. But he was always courteous and friendly towards me, even though he knew I was Jewish. He seemed to like me and trust me. Was he trying to compensate for his anti-Jewish views? Was he conflicted about disliking a group of people but liking individuals of the group? It's easy to be a racist in theory, but harder to hate a breathing human being standing in front of you, especially if he seems like a normal person, just like you.

Of course, there is no logic to racial prejudice. Human beings are naturally social creatures, drawn into interaction with other humans of all races and backgrounds. Racism is a theory based on ignorance which often collapses in practice. The racist is surprised to find someone who belongs to the inferior group who doesn't conform to his image. That should be enough to challenge the stereotype. But he probably learned his ideas in his high chair, he doesn't give them up easily. Instead, he explains his experience with some kind of convoluted rationale: I don't like Them, but this person is different, the exception. He doesn't see the gap in logic. Maybe this person is the only one of Them he has ever met. How many will he have to know before he'll challenge his beliefs?

We humans are consistently inconsistent, creatures of contradiction. We use the beauty of cultural identity for ugly purpose, as an instrument of hatred toward others. How often in history have people left their prayer service where they honoured the god of peace, then ran into the streets to rampage against those who honour the god of peace in a different way?

Each cultural group carries the seeds, if not the fully formed fruit, of animosity toward other groups. This animosity is nourished by feelings of supremacy, the belief that our group is superior to another, and of exclusion, the belief that the other group should be kept apart because they are inferior or evil.

These feelings often lead to the idea of replacement. Because we are superior or they are inferior, we must overcome them, turn them into us, or get rid of them entirely. We believe their religion is outdated or misdirected, ours is the one true faith that must prevail. So we offer them conversion. If they refuse, we expel or destroy them.

Or the other people are backward savages. We must conquer them, civilize them, make them similar to us. We try to bring order to their lives, give them religion, put them to work. It's for their own good, and maybe ours as well—we'll make better use of their land. If they resist, we show them how superior we are through the use of our weapons.

19

THE MOUSE AND THE BEAR

It had just rained and I was walking down the muddy village road stepping around the puddles. An elderly man leaned out his front window and called to me.

"Hey, where you going?"

"For a walk."

"C'mon inside." And he disappeared from the window to open his front door.

His name was August Dick, he was about sixty-five, round and squat, with gleaming black hair. A near-empty pint bottle of Five Star whiskey sat on the kitchen table. It was mid-afternoon in the remote coastal village of Ahminiquis, and August was drinking whiskey from a coffee mug.

I had trouble understanding him; he spoke in words and phrases that didn't always connect. "Too much of it gone now . . . What we, what I see as an elder, people are forgetting . . . Friendly Cove meant a lot of things to our chief . . . had twenty tribes behind him."

In Canada you don't have to be an immigrant to miss the place you come from. You can be a native whose ancestors lived thirty miles away and roamed the lands and seas around you for hundreds of years.

As a journalist working in Victoria, I was chasing the story of native identity on the West Coast and the meeting points between aboriginal culture and the rest of society. It was the summer of 1995, I was approaching fifty and had been living in British Columbia for fifteen years. In the back of my mind, I could see parallels between these people caught between two worlds and my own identity conflicts. I even thought I detected echoes of Hebrew words in the speech of some of the coastal natives, invoking the myth of the lost tribes of Israel.

August Dick's home village of Friendly Cove is a place of great historical significance to British Columbia. It was the ancestral home of the Mowachaht, the native people who greeted Captain James Cook when he arrived in B.C. in 1778. It was the beginning of European society on the West Coast and the beginning of the end of the traditional native way of life.

Forty years ago, the entire Mowachaht tribe moved thirty miles from Friendly Cove up a series of inlets to Ahminiquis at the mouth of the Gold River on the west side of Vancouver Island. This was common practice all over the coast. As small settlements faded away with population decline, the survivors joined together with other native groups. Friendly Cove became a distant place of memories where the Mowachaht go for special ceremonies and summer retreats. But the dream of a revival of the ancient village lived on, a kind of native Zionism. Even young kids of the tribe still talked about "going home" to Friendly Cove.

The new home of the Mowachaht was located in the shadow of a pulp mill that emitted pollutants that poisoned the air and the water. I was told the villagers didn't hang their laundry out to dry because the fumes would eat holes in the cloth. I was also told not to park my car near the mill—particles in the air would corrode the paint job.

Soon after my visit to Ahminiquis, the Mowachaht would be moved again, up to the mountains, still further away from their ancestral home at Friendly Cove. The government would finance the move to a new townsite in the hills behind the town of Gold River, to escape the pollutants from the mill, which are harmful to human health as well as to laundry and the paint on a car.

I asked August about the move to the new village, the third home of his people in the twentieth century. "I belong out here by the ocean, not in the mountains." He stared out the window, as if he could see his home village in the distance.

I glanced at a miniature Indian headdress lying on the table between us.

"Take a look," he said.

I picked it up; red, blue and green beads strung through wire to form a plastic feathered headdress that fit in the palm of my hand.

"You like it?"

"It's nice." It was a trinket, something you might hang on the mirror of your car.

"You want it?"—and before I could answer—"forty dollars."

My eyes flashed on the bottle and I caught myself wondering how many he would buy with forty dollars.

"Oh, no, thanks, but—"

"I made it myself."

"Yes, it's nice, but really, I don't think so."

"Forty dollars."

"Sure, but I can't, really."

"Well take it."

"No, no, that's fine, thanks anyway."

"Take it. For nothing."

"I couldn't, really. It's nice, but—"

"You take it." He found a paper bag and slipped the headdress inside and handed it to me.

Suddenly I was trapped. I was out in the bush and didn't have forty dollars to spare. But if I refused this little sales item that became a gift I would insult him. I had told him I liked it. He stripped away the only barrier to my having it, the money. How could I say no? I took it. I was embarrassed, ashamed.

This little headdress had nothing to do with his culture. The natives on the coast did not wear feathered war bonnets. It was just a little kitchen cottage industry, an old man threading beads onto wire to make souvenirs to sell to visitors.

Up the road, Chief Ambrose Maquinna sold cold pop from a dispenser in his front room. He was the descendant of the powerful Chief Maquinna who ruled over many tribes at Friendly Cove and invited Captain Cook ashore to trade sea otter pelts and cedar masks for metal tools and weapons. These people harpooned thirty-ton whales from dugout canoes and hauled them back to their village and practised secret rituals with wooden carvings of whales and humans to ensure the success of the hunt. The ancient artifacts are all gone, taken away by collectors, destroyed by missionaries or reclaimed by the forest that overgrows everything.

Today, August Dick's headdress hangs from my office window, plastic coloured beads wired together. August Dick is dead now, he died of sadness, I imagine.

The next day I awoke from an afternoon nap and heard the low hum of a voice grumbling from the living room. I was staying in the village at the home of Arnold and Marguerita James and their three children. I'd been given the parents' room, while the rest of the family slept on mattresses in front of the TV. I stepped outside the bedroom and found the house deserted. The voice was the television, which was on twenty-four hours a day, tuned to a Detroit station—sitcoms, murders and a barbecue cooking show. "Now take that steak from the marinade and toss it onto the barbecue," said the man in the apron, his steak sizzling as it hit the grill. I walked over and switched off the set. Ah, quiet.

In a moment, the rumble of a great engine in the distance replaced the noise of the TV. I stepped over to the window and gazed at the plume of smoke drifting from the pulp mill, a mountain rising behind it, grey rock above the treeline.

A few minutes later Arnold came home, a man in his forties with a permanent wince.

"Who turned off the TV?"

I was reluctant to confess.

"Must have been one of the kids," he said and he switched it back on.

The TV was the fire, I thought, and the family slept together in front of the hearth.

I'm not sure what I expected to find at Ahminiquis. I'd read a few books about the culture of the Mowachaht, but when I asked about some of the traditions I drew blank stares. The kids wore hooded sweatshirts with Chicago Bears logos, their culture beamed in through TV satellites.

Do white folks live like they did two hundred years ago? Did I expect the native people would? No, I didn't think they'd be dancing around the fire in cedar bark cloaks. But I came to find out about the people of first contact with Europeans on the coast and I was looking for links to the past. Then, when we went fishing near Friendly Cove, I noticed Arnold aligning his boat with a particular mountain on the horizon to find an undersea channel where the salmon migrate, just like his ancestors did centuries ago, according to the books I've read.

After a few days, I came to realize the artifacts may be gone, but the values were still there. Everyone is related, or acts like they are. Children in the village seem interchangeable, all treated like everyone's own. Friends and neighbours wander in for a chat, for coffee, for a meal. No one asks, "Would you like to stay for dinner?" A plate of food just appears on the table in front of you. These people all belong to the tribe, a word that seems outdated but still appropriate.

These values that remain are a sense of kinship, an attachment to the land and the open-hearted benevolence that leaves doors open to neighbours and extends to a white man from the city sleeping in Arnold and Marguerita's bed.

★

As a child, I never encountered Indians. My only experience of native culture was what I saw in movies or books. Like most boys of my generation, I often played cowboys and Indians. A variation was the Lone Ranger, a game we adapted from the TV show, which I played with my cousin Easor. We both wanted to be the masked hero who shot silver bullets, not his Indian sidekick Tonto, who murmured "Yes, kemosabe," which we took to mean, "Yes, master." Real Indians were in Caughnawaga, the little Mohawk village just outside Montreal, which we knew about but never visited.

I only became aware of natives as real people when I moved to Western Canada in my twenties. They make up a larger percentage of the population in the West, where the land was settled by white people more recently.

You can't walk through the downtown of any major western city without encountering native people. Many of them are struggling to survive and adapt to life in the city, which can be a tough place for a person raised on a reserve way out in the bush.

Gradually I picked up the attitude about natives prevalent among many people in Western Canada. They don't hate them, they feel sorry for them, for their poverty, alcoholism, dislocation. The attitude is, Indians are different, apart, outside the realm of the rest of society. Almost less than human, like wildlife.

The good clean Canadian ideal is that we are not racist. The truth is that some of us are, but we try to hide it. Just ask a native person about getting a job or a place to live in the city, or about relations with police or social workers. Some stores or even gas stations discourage native customers as a matter of practice.

Public services available to everyone else are often denied to natives because different branches of govern-

ment delay and deny and send them away. I witnessed
this myself when I did a study for an aboriginal group on
services available to disabled people in British Columbia. Many a crippled native person who struggles to find
his way to a government office is told, "Go to your band,"
which means "Get lost" in bureaucratic language.

Perhaps the easiest explanation for why native people
are considered outside the realm is that they were never
included in the new society created by the influx of white
people. In the early years, the official policy was assimilation, based on wiping out native culture, turning them
into us. But they were never really accepted into the
greater society, neither on their own terms nor on ours.

Instead of demanding that native people be more like
us, we might turn the mirror around and be more like
them. These people learned to live on these lands over
thousands of years and could teach us some of the skills
and values that allowed them to survive and flourish.
That might make us feel more at home, more at peace,
rather than displaced Europeans trying to impose our
beliefs on the New World. It's something I've tried myself with mixed results. I own a native button blanket
sewn by my wife and a headband I weaved from cedar
bark. And I've travelled deep in the wilderness practising
the old ways with the Indians—where I discovered how
unIndian I really am.

On the West Coast, if you want to be a native, you have
to learn how to fillet a salmon. How to gut and slice the
fish in seconds, removing all the succulent, pink meat in
two long strips and leaving the bones and intestines behind. The natives on this coast have survived cold, lean
winters on dried salmon for thousands of years. Today,

they still catch salmon spawning in fresh water in the fall and cut and dry them for winter food.

There is no deeper wilderness on the British Columbia coast than the Kitlope, a million acres of towering forests, whitecapped mountains, blue-green rivers and sparkling Kitlope Lake. It's located halfway between the northern end of Vancouver Island and the southern tip of Alaska, a six-hour boat ride from the native town of Kitamaat. I travelled there, among the jumble of islands and inlets of the Inside Passage, to explore this spectacular wilderness with the Haisla, the native people of the area. It was early fall and the Haisla were catching sockeye salmon at the lake, butchering the fish and drying the fillets in a smoke shack at a camp a few miles downriver. Over the course of a week we saw no other sign of humanity—no boats, no planes and no cars because there are no roads in the Kitlope.

I was here to research a story on the struggle to save the Kitlope from logging, but was soon recruited to help with the salmon harvest. At a long wooden table under an overhang of trees, an elderly native woman with a kitchen knife instructed me in the art of filleting.

She picked up a fat sockeye about the size of a loaf of bread. "Make sure the knife is sharp." It was, gliding through the salmon's belly in one smooth stroke. In a flash, the guts spilled onto the table and she turned the blade on the back of the fish.

"Now cut, don't saw." With a few strokes, she slid the knife through the back down toward the belly and the meat fell away from the backbone. "Now the other side." She was working so fast I could barely follow, let alone remember how to copy her method. She laid the two strips of pink meat at the side of the table and tossed the entrails into a bucket. She reached for a fresh salmon from the pile and handed it to me. "Give it a try." She went to another table to continue cutting.

I flipped over the slippery sockeye, inserted the knife in the anus and started slicing toward the gills, trying to hold the fish by the tail. The guts came out in bloody sacks and tubes, the miracle of life deep at sea spilled into a waste bucket like so much sewage. I tried to mimic her slices down the back of the fish but my strokes were tentative and uneven. I produced some good fillets and a few hacked pieces and useless thin strips. I was working at about a quarter the speed of the half dozen people around me, but no one seemed to notice.

As we cut, we were plagued by hordes of flying insects—wasps, hornets, flies and other nasties—buzzing in the air and landing on the fish, on the tables, on our hands and faces. I gave up trying to wave them away, just shook my head like a horse when they got close to my eyes or mouth.

I was working on one piece, trying to hold the fish and cut as close to the bone as possible. The blade sliced clean through the pink flesh—and into the pink flesh of my forefinger. Pain shot through my finger as I dropped the knife and grabbed my left hand. I rushed to a tub of water to wash out the wound, blood dripping on the ground. I stood there bent over the tub holding my finger as my blood flowed into the water in small liquid clouds. What would I do now, I wondered. This was a deep cut, and I was six hours from a doctor. My mind raced—infection, panic, blood and more blood.

Another Haisla woman came by and led me to the edge of the bush.

"You see that tree over there?"

I nodded as she gestured at a cedar. The tree had a wedge cut into it and was bleeding sap.

"Go take some of the sap and put it on the cut."

What choice did I have? I walked over to the tree and carefully applied the sticky golden liquid to the cut with my good hand. The bleeding stopped instantly, the sap closing the wound like glue. The throbbing pain subsided. The tree's blood had closed the cut and stopped the flow of my blood. I took a few deep breaths and went back to the filleting tables, using nine fingers. Over the next few days I applied more sap. The wound healed in about half the time I expected and left no scar.

The next day, I joined a small group travelling by boat to Kitlope Lake to bring back fresh supplies of sockeye. Hauling in the salmon was hard, heavy work, but more exciting than cutting. The Haisla laid nets in the lake where the salmon spawned and then came back a few days later to haul in the fish trapped in the twine. Three of us drew in the net, straining as we pulled on the mass of nylon netting and dozens of eight-pound fish. The trickiest part was grasping and untangling the slippery salmon, some still struggling for life. Each fish was caught in several places in netting so thin it was barely visible. At one point, bright pink eggs the size of pearls spilled out from the bottom of a writhing fish. I caught the salty eggs in my hand and gobbled them, feeling like a wild man of the woods and drawing strange stares from my co-workers.

Back at the camp on the river, the putrid smell of fish guts was attracting more than flies. A big black bear was prowling the area looking for an easy meal. The animal

came close to the cutting tables several times and a young
native hauled out his high-calibre rifle. He took careful
aim and the shots echoed through the valley as he fired
above the bear's head to scare it away.

That night, a group of us were huddling around the
campfire trading stories. As the flames began to subside,
we heard a big animal thrashing in the woods. Two of us
stood up to shine a flashlight at the sound. I heard the
crunch of breaking branches and a grunting snarl. I could
barely make out a black form thirty feet away in the bush.
We doused the flames and headed off to bed rather than
meet the bear in the dark.

As we lay in our bunk beds in the small cabin, the
conversation turned to the inevitable bear-attack stories.
One man told of a bear that put a paw through a cabin
wall, climbed in and tore the place apart. Even more exotic creatures were believed to live in these woods. One
elderly Haisla told us his father shot a sasquatch, the
mythical ape man of the northwest, fifty years ago on
this river.

Soon I drifted off, but it was a fretful sleep. A big bear
was tearing through the walls of the cabin and attacking
us. The dream dissolved as I awoke in the night. As I
turned in my bed, I heard a rustling noise that sounded
like the bear stirring in the woods. I lay there frozen, and
then the sound was suddenly inside the cabin, across the
room! I listened with a dry mouth, my heart accelerat-
ing, planning my escape. Finally the noise stopped, but I
stayed awake in the darkness for a while, my ears alert.

When I got up in the morning, I wondered if any of
my cabin-mates had heard the rustling sound in the night.
Before I could ask, I discovered the source of the noise:

At the Qatuwas canoe festival in the summer of 1993 in Bella Bella, where the chief invited 1,500 strangers to his wedding.

a mouse trapped at the bottom of a wastebasket nibbling on melon rinds. I emptied him into the woods and never mentioned my fearful spell to the others. People in the wild sometimes confuse deer, humans or even tree stumps for bear, but perhaps this was the first time someone mistook a mouse for a black bear.

I had a lot to learn about native traditions, more than I could in a week in the woods. There was a wide gap between these native people who still lived largely on the land and my own experience on the streets of Canadian cities. But the gap was more than cutting salmon and learning to identify wildlife; it was a way of thinking that extended to treatment of fellow humans, including strangers to native communities like myself.

On my way in to the Kitlope, I had been stranded in Kitamaat, the north coast village and central home of the Haisla. When I arrived at the dock, the boat I was supposed to travel in was full and two people were asked to stay behind: Alison Davis, a young anthropology student from Vancouver, and me. The boat would return for another trip to the Kitlope in three days.

So what would I do in Kitamaat for three days? And where would I stay? There wasn't even a corner grocery, let alone a hotel in the little village. The white town of Kitimat—same pronunciation, different spelling—was five miles away, but we had no vehicle. Alison knew someone in the native village. We walked over and I met Sylvia Wilson, a shy, slight woman in her early thirties. She lived in a small two-storey home with her four children, Chris, Amber, Patrick and Tannis. As casual as offering a cup of coffee, Sylvia opened up her home. The kids moved in with each other and Alison and I were given their bedrooms.

This has happened to me three times in remote native communities. At Sylvia's place in Kitamaat, at Arnold and Marguerita's house in Ahminiquis, and at the home of the Carpenter family in Bella Bella, a remote, misty village on the mid-coast. In Bella Bella I attended the Qatuwas, a gathering of more than thirty tribes at the first native canoe festival on the West Coast in a hundred years. The local Heiltsuk people accommodated 1,500 paddlers and visitors from Alaska to California at the week-long festival. There were seventeen guests at the Carpenter home, including photographer Brett Lowther and myself in their daughter's bedroom. She went to live with friends and the parents slept on the floor in the living room.

These people owed me nothing. And they expected nothing, certainly no great thanks or payment. It was just what they did. A stranger on the road needed a bed and they gave him one. And breakfast every morning. I remember the Carpenters casually cooking pancakes for twenty at seven a.m. Naturally, without strain or fuss.

The first day those 1,500 strangers arrived in Bella Bella for the canoe festival happened to be the day the chief, Edwin Newman, was getting married. The chief announced at a community gathering that every one of those people was invited to the wedding reception. And they all showed up the next evening and enjoyed a seafood feast of salmon, halibut, cod, dried herring eggs and eulachon oil, a strong, smelly fish oil used as a condiment.

In white society, we would call this hospitality. But this word doesn't seem to fit the native experience. To me, it just seemed like a natural enfolding into the family. Suddenly, I was part of the Wilson family, the James family, the Carpenters. The fact that I was white didn't seem to matter. At Sylvia Wilson's home, the doors were always open, friends stopping by to sit with her and drink Labrador tea. Neighbourhood kids would casually drop into the James home and play with toys, watch TV or raid the refrigerator as if it was their own house.

The native people know the secrets of living on the land, including the code of providing for people travelling through their territory. Some of this knowledge has been lost in recent generations, but much of it remains. Native people wouldn't have survived for thousands of years in B.C. if they needed a doctor every time they cut their finger. Or if they depended on the grocery for food or hotels for a place to stay. They thrived on this coast for a hundred centuries without consuming most of the forests and most of the fish, which we have managed to do in a hundred years. They have some important skills and lessons to teach us. If only we'd stop our busyness long enough to listen.

2 0

NEW COUNTRY

The house sways gently as the wind rocks the trees. All around me is a curtain of evergreen branches and beyond that only glimpses of sky. The branches are so close, I could just about step out onto them, if they would hold my weight. The raccoons do just that, walking in and out of this small cabin through the second-storey window.

This is the old-growth forest, the natural splendour of British Columbia that attracts hikers and adventurers from around the world. My friend Andrew Struthers built this cabin in the trees outside Tofino on the west coast of Vancouver Island and became a forest creature himself. He called his home the pyramid, two small rooms— a living area downstairs and a sleeping loft upstairs. He had no running water, no electricity and no road access, just a muddy trail that snaked over roots and rocks through the forest. When he built the cabin, he walked that trail many times a day carrying tools, building supplies, panes of glass and a wood stove on his back.

From his little shack in the bush, Andrew developed his skills as a writer and an artist. He drew a cartoon series called The Cheese Club, which he sold all over North America. And with a tiny manual typewriter, he wrote magazine articles and a book about life in Tofino called *The Green Shadow*.

This was the mid-1990s, Andrew was in his early thirties, built like a barrel, with an impish grin and red hair that he shaved off when he started going bald. He wore a dangling earring in his left ear and exotic clothes. He showed up at my office in Victoria at *Monday Magazine* wearing an American flag for a hat. It had blown off the back of a boat that was visiting Tofino.

Andrew lived a kind of double life between the idyllically peaceful pyramid and the fish-processing plant where he worked on the line, butchering thousands of salmon raised in fish farms. He was known as the master slasher for his skill at cutting out the gills of the fish with a flick of the wrist. He shared his home in the woods with his daughter Pasheabel, a little sprite who scrambled over rocky cliffs at the beach with alarming speed.

Many people would consider isolation in a cabin with no modern conveniences a hardship, but Andrew was living his dream. He was surrounded by nature and he was "off the grid"—no rent, no mortgage, no utility bills, no car payments. In the morning, he hitchhiked to his job at the fish plant. When he wasn't working, he wrote or drew cartoons or surfed for hours in a wetsuit in the breaking waves off the beach.

Andrew later moved to Victoria, to a one-bedroom apartment with no kitchen and a bathroom down the hall, where he launched his career as a filmmaker and painted houses on the side to pay the rent. He has lived in various parts of the world and adapts easily to new cultures and circumstances. Born in Scotland, he lived with his family in Uganda when he was a young child. Their home was in the mountains in a village called Jinja above Lake Victoria. He remembers gazelles running beside his father's car and an angry hippopotamus chasing the family in a dugout canoe. Later, they moved back to Scotland, then to British Columbia, first to Prince George, then to Victoria. At 24, Andrew went to Japan for two years, then returned to Canada. Andrew is of one ethnic background, but the experiences of Scotland, Africa, Japan and British Columbia are essential parts of his character. He incorporates all the cultures of the places where he's lived—and others—into his view of the world. He has read more stories in translation by Yiddish writer Isaac Bashevis Singer than anyone else I know.

Andrew's mixed identity emerges in his writing, his thinking and the films he is making. One is called *Aeon*, about a time thousands of years in the future when the natural world has reclaimed the earth and all races of humankind have melded into one. He calls himself "a planet baby," someone who identifies with world culture instead of a particular ethnic group. Andrew became a planet baby through life experience, but many younger people today were born with a mixed ethnic identity.

The notion of Canadians as English, French, Italian or East Indian ignores the reality that some of us are all of the above. Immigration today accounts for half of the country's population growth, five times as much as when I was growing up. It was only natural that some of these

immigrants from all over the world would marry each
other and raise children of mixed background. The old
idea of drawing your identity from the place of origin of
your grandparents is fading away in this country. The
new Canada sees beyond race, religion and ethnic background when it looks in the mirror.

My own experience in Canada today is so radically
different from the place I grew up in, I sometimes wonder if it's the same country. In many ways, it isn't. My
friends and even family members are of various ethnic
backgrounds and we often celebrate each other's festi-
vals and holidays. This is our birthright as human beings
in a modern, evolved society: to be Us *in* Them, to be
rooted in our own traditions and to interweave with other
cultures around us.

People today feel free to hold firm to their tribe of
origin or to cross over to other groups. White kids become Rastafarians, anglos become francophones, Christians convert to Judaism. About a third of the leadership
of my synagogue is made up of people who converted,
many of their own conviction, not because they married
a Jewish person.

You don't have to travel or have parents from opposite sides of the globe to share Andrew's world view. You
can absorb it through the Internet, television or other
media and cultural exchange. It's especially prevalent on
MTV, where young people of mixed or undetermined
identity perform for people like themselves around the
world in an endless loop of music, hype and feedback.
The emerging mentality is that we are all one nation.
People like Andrew didn't invent global consciousness,
but they were the first generation to be born into it.

Perhaps the light clicked on when we saw the pictures of the earth from outer space, or the immense cloud rising above Hiroshima, or the twin towers collapsing in New York. Certainly, communication links us with every part of the world and by extension, every person in the world. This is a new phenomenon, expanding as the information age continues to unfold around us.

In Canada, diversity and tolerance have moved beyond ethnicity, race and religion to include concepts like gender and sexual orientation. The idea that we can all step forward and openly take our place in society is widely accepted in this country.

I have lived my life between cultures, the one I was raised in and the greater North American culture around me. I have grown to believe I am a citizen of the world, that the future of the earth lies in people of different backgrounds coexisting and finding solutions together, not tightening the circle around their own group to exclude outsiders. Whether the ghetto was enforced or embraced, for centuries Jews lived among themselves, practising their faith and studying the religious teachings behind closed doors.

The test for people like me is whether we can live in the greater world and maintain our identities. I wonder if this is possible outside the enclosure of the isolated Jewish community. I suspect that Judaism survived this long because of the separation that compelled us to identify as a distinct people.

In *Constantine's Sword*, an excellent book about the Catholic Church and the Jews, scholar James Carroll says Jews made up ten per cent of the Roman Empire two thousand years ago and should have naturally reached a population of 200 million in modern times. But they didn't. There are only fourteen million Jews in the world today. We are the remnants, the survivors. Those 186 million missing Jews are the testament to persistent persecution by the Romans and the Christian and Muslim kingdoms and empires that followed.

Fourteen million is less than the population of each of the seven largest cities of the world. Less than the population of Madagascar or Cameroon. About two tenths of one per cent of the world's population.

To me, this is one of the great mysteries of the world. Any group of people that dates back four thousand years should have grown to several hundred million people or disappeared entirely. The fact that the Jewish people still exist today, but in such tiny numbers, is beyond comprehension. It's like discovering a small patch of red sand on the edge of a beach and finding it again a lifetime later, after all those seasons of high tides, winds and storms. Such improbabilities make you wonder about divine destiny.

The human tendency is to believe that what always was always will be. Yet the survival of the Jewish people is by no means assured in the twenty-first century. The population outside Israel of 8.6 million is declining due to low birth rate and assimilation. Experts predict it may decrease by fifty per cent within a generation. The Jewish people must be placed on the endangered list of human tribes, a small remnant of a group still struggling to survive against all odds.

2 1

A LOCAL BOY

In the airport lounge, I spy a large man with fleshy
cheeks and lips, watchful eyes, grey tones to his skin.
In a moment I recognize him. Sydney Pfeiffer, one of
my classmates at Adath Israel school in Montreal. I
haven't spoken to him in 40 years, but I catch his eye as
he approaches me.

Ah yes, he remembers and we shake hands. We are in
Toronto waiting for the 1 a.m. direct flight to Israel. I am
travelling with Jen to visit my mother, now widowed and
alone. He is going to see friends and clients. I will be
staying on Kfar Menachem, south of Tel Aviv. He will be
at a hotel in Jerusalem, within walking distance of the
Western Wall, so he can arrive on foot to pray on Shabbes
at the most sacred site of the Jewish religion. God comes
before any threat of terrorism. He wears a knitted wool
kipa as he did when he was a child. It seems worn and
shaped to his head and I almost imagine it is the same
one, except of course it would no longer fit. His *kipa* set

him apart from most of us at Adath Israel as the son of a religious family.

Sydney proudly tells me of his children—this one in this profession, that one in that university or married to this prominent person. And his work? He is a tax lawyer, with degrees in both law and accountancy. His office is on St. Alexander Street in Montreal. I tell him I worked on the same lower downtown street thirty years ago at Canadian Press and he remembers the building.

"So how is living in Montreal after all these years?"

"It's a very nice city."

With its mix of Old World charm and New World vitality, Montreal is a comfortable fit for people of European background. Sydney's family came from Germany; his father slipped away before the war, ahead of Hitler's death grasp. Despite all that history, many German Jews still seem very German, cultured, formal, elitist.

"You must speak French well."

"Yes. You know I served for many years on the Outremont council." I did know that; I still stayed in the old neighbourhood with my friend Dennis Trudeau from CP days when I visited Montreal. Sydney was certainly the only Jew, perhaps the only anglophone, on the Outremont city council. He still lives in the neighbourhood, in a grand old stone house just a few blocks from my old family home on Clinton Avenue.

"And how's business?"

"I can't complain."

"Who are your clients?"

"They're mostly French Canadian. They come to me with their problems and I try to solve them."

Very matter-of-fact, yet for me, a product of the old Montreal, this is surprising. He is identifiably Jewish; he wears the sign on his head. But French Canadians who are fighting the tax collector are eager to hire him because he's good at what he does.

But then I realize, of course his clientele are Québécois. Who else but French Canadians are going to need a tax lawyer in downtown Montreal? They make up the large majority of Montrealers. He couldn't survive on St. Alexander Street as a lawyer specializing in tax cases with a Jewish clientele.

Am I naive to be surprised? How much has my native city changed over all these years? How comfortable with one another have the Jews and the Québécois become? How much water has flowed under the bridge, washing away years of distrust?

I remember the old nationalist phrase *Le Québec aux Québécois*. Was that idea abandoned—or was it broadened to include people like Sydney Pfeiffer? Like the city he lives in and the people who live there, he is French-speaking, immersed in tradition and culturally connected to Europe. Is that enough to be counted among the greater tribe?

Sydney leans over and removes his siddur, his prayer book, from his carry-on luggage. He looks settled, content. He was heavy as a child and he is heavy today, about the same shape and twice the size. I imagine him burrowed in his humble office in the grimy part of downtown Montreal, poring over tax records as if he was studying the Talmud, a Québécois client at his elbow, waiting to hear his words of wisdom. *"Y'a pas de problème, Monsieur . . ."*

Thirty years ago I left Montreal and he stayed. It's easy to say we saw the city differently and we both made the right decision. But sometimes I wonder. As beautiful and vibrant as ever, Montreal still feels like home when I'm there.

And so I go back, sometimes for work and sometimes just to visit friends and family and stir up old memories. On one trip to Quebec, I was driving to the Laurentians to gather research for a story. I was living in British Columbia, land of the biggest trees, the grandest forests in Canada. North of Montreal, I pulled over to the side of the highway, got out and stared at the woods. They looked incredibly beautiful. The leafy oaks, the white birch, the nodding evergreens, small trees in mixed stands, this was my forest as I remembered it, like the woods behind our home on Fourteen Island Lake. I knew the feeling of exile. I am still a son of Quebec, but at a distance.

Back in the city, I strolled through a park in lower Outremont. I heard the sound of children playing, calls and laughter at a near distance. At the far entrance to the park stood a large stone monument, the names of the war dead etched into the slab. And there on the side, Sydney Tafler, my father's cousin, the man I'm named after, an RCAF flying officer shot down over Germany in 1945. How could you be more closely tied to a place than to find your name carved in stone on a war monument?

It's the split mindset of a place I once called home and now only visit. The familiar, the house on Clinton where we lived, and the unfamiliar, the strangers who live there now. I drive the streets of Outremont craning my neck like a tourist returning to a favourite city. Yes, that was the corner store on Rockland, a different name, but still there. The field behind our school where we hopped the fence to put pennies on the railroad tracks—gone, replaced by a hockey rink and an overpass.

"I know you." A man my age wearing a dark suit and tie approaches me on the lawn of the church.

I turn to him, meeting his eyes through his dark-framed glasses. I don't recognize him but I smile. "From where?"

"You're from around here, aren't you?" He speaks English seasoned with a French-Canadian accent.

"I used to be."

"You were one of those kids that hung out at my father's drugstore—DeGuire's."

My mind flashed back forty years. The sign above the drugstore window with the familiar name, DeGuire. The quiet man, the pharmacist in the white smock behind the counter, rows of merchandise, a mirror, a candy case.

"That was a long time ago. How do you remember?" I study his face, still no recognition.

"You're a local boy. I remember you." I watch as he joins his wife and walks away.

So you *can* go home again, I thought. I was throwing a football with my friend Dennis and his son Sam on the church lawn on a Sunday morning when the man appeared at the end of the service.

This was my old neighbourhood in Outremont, just a few blocks from the house on Clinton. DeGuire's was on Van Horne, the main shopping thoroughfare in the area. The store is gone now, just a memory invoked by the son of the owner. When I was a boy, my friends and I would stop in on our way home from school and buy five-cent chocolate bars.

I never knew Mr. DeGuire had a son, but I suppose he

noticed us at the counter, the local school kids stopping in at the store. And many years later, through all of life's changes, he recognized me as a middle-aged man throwing a football on the church lawn. I was amazed. How could he remember me? Was it me specifically that looked familiar, or was I one of a type?

A local boy, he called me. It's a degree of acceptance I never had back then from kids like Mr. DeGuire's son. I was *les autres*, one of the others, avoided, kept apart. But now we had both grown older and the world had changed around us, and we had changed as well.

This was my city, this is my past. But my tribe is dispersed, replaced by new tribes. I still hold the remorse of the exile, but it's suddenly soothed by this recognition from the son of the pharmacist, the French kid I never knew. Those few words on the lawn of the church felt like an acknowledgment of who I am, who we are, after all those years. And I remembered another churchyard a half-century ago, where my sister and I were chased away by a nun in a black habit.

Back home in Victoria, I step outside on a cool spring day and smell the salt air drifting in from the Pacific. I walk down my street to the bluffs overlooking the water and gaze at the mountains in the distance. It's a moment of quiet reflection in the midst of a workday. Life is about making peace, about coming to terms with your decisions, the place where you live, the people around you, near and far.

And I think about those who are gone, the people who once formed my family and tribe. Their absence makes those who are left all the more important, a vital link to who we were in the past and who we are today.

★

"Do you feel the snow on your face, Mom?"

"Yes."

"How does it feel?"

"Wet."

On the edge of the Pacific on the southern tip of Vancouver Island, the snow is often wet when it falls, usually only once or twice a winter, if at all. Children race to Beacon Hill Park to slide down on their toboggans, but many older folks stay inside and wait for the snow to melt.

But Sarah Tafler didn't want to stay inside. At 87, she hadn't seen snow in thirty-three years and she didn't want to miss it. So I pushed her in her wheelchair down Douglas Street toward the beach, where we could see the snow falling from a grey sky into the swirling ocean. The small flakes touched her cheeks and we left tracks in the snow.

Many times when we visited her in Israel, she told me she wished she could feel the snow on her face, just one more time.

She wanted to be near her family, and she wanted to be back in a place where people spoke English, the language of her childhood. On the kibbutz, disabled after a stroke and several falls, she had moved into the old folks' home, called *chadrei cholim*, the sick rooms. At meals she sat at a table with two sweet elderly women, Mushka and Fradka, but she shared not a word of conversation with them. They spoke no English and Sarah had lost her Hebrew to old age.

For all those years living in Israel, she had missed her family. But with Dad gone, Mom's loneliness had turned to desperation. At a stage of life where some people no longer take you seriously, she asked us to take her back to Canada. Some friends and relatives argued that she should stay on the kibbutz, where she had her social circle and good geriatric care. She had broken her hip in her last fall. Moving Sarah in her condition just a few months later would be a great risk, a potential disaster. But living alone far from family was already a disaster. I knew I couldn't deny her wish.

Moving an elderly Jewish person, my own mother, out of the land of Israel was as much a psychic struggle as a difficult task of travelling with a disabled person. For centuries, Jewish people yearned to go back to the promised land. The idea of removing a woman in her late years, returning her to exile, provoked conflict and anxiety within me. To Jews, being connected with Israel is so important that a handful of earth from Jerusalem is sprinkled into the graves of each person buried outside the homeland.

Then I remembered the story of my birth, the struggle my mother endured and endured again and how that story grew to symbolize her love and sacrifice for me. Now we would struggle together again to bring her back to Canada in the summer of 2003.

This move meant she would leave Abe behind, forever. They always assumed they would be buried next to each other. I went alone again to the cemetery on the edge of the kibbutz. He had died three years before and the flowers and succulents planted near his grave had taken root and flourished. I stood by his headstone, his name etched in Hebrew and English, and dropped a pebble, a Jewish symbol of remembrance. This time I said nothing. I thought of my father, his life, his dream and my love for him. I remembered his tenderness and his strength. Life is for the living, I thought. She stood by you for sixty-five years, now she will be near her children. It's where you live that matters, not where your body lies when you die. I knew he would agree.

A few days later, in the dead of night, we boarded the plane at Tel Aviv airport, my wife Jen at the aisle, my mother Sarah in the middle, me at the window. I looked out at the dark runway and then shut my eyes and wept as the plane lifted off. We were leaving home and going home again.